Norfolk & Virginia Beach: Historical Guide for Travelers

American Cities History Guidebook Series

Henry Church

Published by Fiel LLC, 2023.

While every precaution has been taken in the preparation of this book, the publisher assumes no responsibility for errors or omissions, or for damages resulting from the use of the information contained herein.

NORFOLK & VIRGINIA BEACH: HISTORICAL GUIDE FOR TRAVELERS

First edition. September 8, 2023.

Copyright © 2023 Henry Church.

ISBN: 979-8223533832

Written by Henry Church.

Also by Henry Church

American Cities History Guidebook Series
Charlottesville, Virginia: Historical Guide for Travelers
Williamsburg, Virginia: Historical Guide for Travelers
Richmond, Virginia: Historical Guide for Travelers
Norfolk & Virginia Beach: Historical Guide for Travelers
Winchester, Virginia: Historical Guide for Travelers
Baltimore, Maryland: Historical Guide for Travelers
Dover, Delaware: Historical Guide for Travelers
Arlington, Virginia: Historical Guide for Travelers

Table of Contents

Introduction

The history of Norfolk and Virginia Beach, Virginia, a city that has seen the creation of heroes, the rise and fall of empires, and the passage of time, is as illustrious as the area that surrounds it. Its story, which is intertwined with the history of America itself, is one of tenacity, inventiveness, adversity, and triumph. More than just a place on a map, Norfolk and Virginia Beach serve as a physical reminder of America's past, from its infancy to the present.

This book examines Norfolk and Virginia Beach's early years, significant historical turning moments, and the people who gave it life in an effort to unravel the intricate web of the region's past. Each chapter will take you on a journey through a particular era or facet of Norfolk and Virginia Beach's development. In this tour, we'll retrace the steps of the first settlers, encounter the inhabitants' revolutionary fervor, see the challenges posed by civil wars and societal shifts, and take in the technical and cultural zeniths that have formed the city in the twenty-first century.

Through the prism of time, we'll examine the architectural marvels of Norfolk and Virginia Beach, their cultural influences, and the economic forces that have propelled their growth. We'll study about the social movements that originated in or became stronger in Norfolk and Virginia Beach, and we'll get to know the people who made those places famous.

The story of Norfolk and Virginia Beach, however, is not simply about looking back; it is also about understanding the present and imagining the future. As we explore the history of Norfolk and Virginia Beach, we'll also shine light on the current problems and innovations the city is confronting, giving readers a glimpse into the city's potential future.

Regardless matter whether you're a native wondering about your town, a student interested in its past, or a visitor eager to learn more about this American jewel, this book offers a thorough and fascinating tour of Norfolk and Virginia Beach's history. Let's embark on this historical trip to discover more about the incidents and legacies that have made Norfolk and Virginia Beach, Virginia into the city that it is today.

Chapter 1: Native Tribes of Norfolk and Virginia Beach

Before Norfolk and Virginia Beach became what they are today, the area was a diverse mix of estuaries, woods, and coastal plains where native cultures thrived for generations. The first chapters of the lengthy history of the area were written by their lives, which were intricately entwined with the land, the water, and one another.

One of the most significant tribes in this area, the Chesepian Tribe, lived mostly along the productive banks of the Elizabeth and Lynnhaven rivers. The Chesepians, who were a part of the larger Powhatan Confederacy, were particularly well-suited to their coastal habitat. The yehakins, or longhouses, that made up their villages were frequently found close to where the rivers met the bay. These were mostly constructed from local resources including grasses, bark, and saplings.

The Chesepians and other tribes in the area used artistically carved boats fashioned from big trees to assist trade and transportation. These canoes were more than just functional; they represented the close connection between the Chesepian people and their aquatic surroundings. Fish, clams, oysters, and crabs made up substantial sections of their food, which was largely derived from these waterways. They engaged in a combination of cultivation and hunting on land. Their main sources of food were the "Three Sisters," or corn, beans, and squash. The abundant areas made it possible to hunt small mammals and game like deer and wild turkey.

Culturally, the Chesepians shared the love for environment and spirituality shared by other tribes of the Powhatan Confederacy. They honored the passing of the seasons, life's milestones, and their symbiotic relationship with the environment through ceremonies, dances, and rituals. The rituals were crucial for preserving social harmony within the tribe and for fostering relationships with other tribes.

The peace and quiet of Chesepian existence, nevertheless, was about to be disturbed. The early 17th century saw the arrival of European settlers, which had a profound impact on the area's dynamics. Initially friendly, the Chesepians would soon come into conflict with the immigrants, which would cause conflicts, shifts in territorial boundaries, and finally a change in the region's cultural and societal makeup.

Chapter 2: Early Settlers and Their Stories

The horizon's silhouette started to change as dawn broke over the lush plains of what would become Norfolk and Virginia Beach. Beginning to appear on the seas were ships with impressive sails carrying settlers from other regions. These early European settlers—most of whom were English—were attracted by stories of a "New World" brimming with potential and opportunity.

In 1607, the first group of these settlers arrived in Jamestown. Over time, as they continued to travel in pursuit of productive land and prosperous opportunities, they inexorably came into contact with the local Chesepian Tribe and the larger Powhatan Confederacy.

Adam Thoroughgood, an Englishman who arrived in Virginia as an indentured servant in the 1620s, was one of the most renowned early settlers. Thoroughgood overcame early adversity to finally rise to prominence in the Virginia colony. He had acquired a grant of more than 5,000 acres by 1634, when he built plantations and made a substantial contribution to the creation of what is today known as Norfolk. He is frequently given credit for renaming several local locations, notably Lynnhaven, after locations in his native country.

Stories of Coexistence and Conflict: At first, there was a mixture of trade, cooperation, and intermittent confrontations between the settlers and the aboriginal tribes. The Indians contributed their agricultural methods, and in return, the Europeans introduced them to their farming implements. Both parties gained knowledge through the exchange. Conflicts, however, were inevitable as the number of settlers increased their quest for land. Conflicts over possession of land, access to resources, and misunderstandings were frequent. These conflicts grew throughout time, leading to important occasions like the Anglo-Powhatan Wars.

Land and Economy: The region's potential for agriculture, particularly tobacco farming, was immediately recognized by the early European settlers. Tobacco quickly developed into the colony's main cash crop thanks to the fertile and loamy soil of the Chesapeake. The growth of plantations also increased the need for workers. Indentured servitude was used to satisfy this demand at first, and the terrible transatlantic slave trade later filled the gap.

Despite the conflicts, there was a cultural interchange going on. European architectural styles, customs, and religions were introduced by settlers. Churches, a vital component of European towns and cities, started to appear everywhere. The area began to gradually change, with towns developing into active communities.

Challenges did, however, accompany advancement. Along with territory disputes, diseases, strange weather conditions, and sporadic food shortages posed hazards to the settlers. The history of the area is deeply rooted in tales of their tenacity, inventiveness, and resiliency.

The formerly sparse villages became denser as the years progressed into decades. The foundation for Norfolk and Virginia Beach's future cities was formed by the blending of cultures, the pioneering spirit of the settlers, and the rich heritage of the indigenous tribes.

Chapter 3: Norfolk and Virginia Beach in the Colonial Era

For the region that is now Norfolk and Virginia Beach, the Colonial Era marked the beginning of an era of transformation. Early settlers' original settlements developed into more structured communities as the 17th century went on, and they were important elements of the colony's political, social, and economic landscape.

The English presence in the area was obvious by the middle of the 1600s. Given its advantageous location along the Elizabeth River, Norfolk in particular developed into a prominent colonial port. Due to this, trade between the colony and the English homeland as well as other European countries flourished there as well. Norfolk became one of Virginia's wealthiest towns as a result of the exportation of goods like tobacco, lumber, and agricultural products as well as the importation of European goods like textiles, tools, and luxury goods.

Due to its proximity to the Atlantic, Virginia Beach developed became a hub for ships traveling to and from Europe. Its placement was crucial since it provided a lookout and point of defense against potential maritime threats during times of strife.

Both regions' economies were primarily reliant on plantations. The agricultural landscape was dominated by tobacco, also known as "green gold." However, the enormous prosperity of the tobacco industry came at a high price. The labor-intensive crop caused a greater reliance on African slaves, permanently altering the demographics and socioeconomic structure of the area. By the end of the 17th century, African slaves made up a sizeable section of the local population, and in certain cases, they moved from being only laborers to being expert artisans and craftspeople.

The social structure in colonial times was hierarchical. Plantation owners and affluent merchants were at the top, followed by small farmers and craftspeople. The lowest tiers were made up of indentured laborers and slaves from Africa. In determining how the settlers lived their daily lives, religion was a significant factor. As the colony's official religion, Anglicanism had a lot of power. Although it dominated, other religious movements, such Baptists and Quakers, started to gain ground despite occasionally being persecuted for their beliefs.

In the colonial era, education was a luxury, frequently reserved for the affluent. The demand for education, however, increased as societies grew larger. Rich households first hired private tutors, but by the early 18th century, primitive schools started to appear.

As the 18th century got underway, rumblings of opposition to British rule became more audible. Given their importance, Norfolk and Virginia Beach were hardly the only places to hear these rumblings. The burning of Norfolk by British forces in reaction to colonial resistance in 1776 was only one example of how tensions between the colonies and the British crown reached their peak.

Norfolk and Virginia Beach had experienced enormous expansion, prosperity, and instability by the end of the Colonial Era. Their development into important parts of the Virginia colony from fledgling outposts paved the way for their participation in the upcoming Revolutionary War and the creation of a new country.

Chapter 4: Important Landmarks and their History

Numerous historical sites dot the landscapes of Norfolk and Virginia Beach, bearing witness to centuries of development, growth, and transition. Every building, no matter how grand or simple, tells a tale of the people, occasions, and historical periods that have influenced the region's identity.

St. Paul's Episcopal Church, Norfolk: Built in the 1730s, St. Paul's Episcopal Church is one of Norfolk's oldest structures. One of its bricks has the mark of a cannonball from the Revolutionary War, leaving history imprinted on the building's very walls. Through wars, flames, and the shifting sands of history, the church has stood as a steadfast symbol of faith.

The magnificent brick Lynnhaven House in Virginia Beach, constructed around 1725, is a prime example of early Georgian design. The mansion, which belonged to the illustrious Thoroughgood family, offers a glimpse into colonial aristocratic life in Virginia with its elaborate woodwork and brick patterns.

The Ferry Plantation House in Virginia Beach was built on land that was originally granted by King Charles I of England in 1642. The current structure, which dates to the 1830s, has been a courthouse, a school, and even a plantation mansion. Local lore even purports that the hotel's rooms are haunted by ghosts.

The General Douglas MacArthur Memorial in Norfolk is a monument to his life and accomplishments. It is located in the center of Norfolk. There are several items from both World Wars and the Korean War inside its walls. In addition, it serves as the location of General MacArthur and his wife's ultimate burial place.

The third-oldest lighthouse in the United States is located at Virginia Beach and overlooks the point where the Chesapeake Bay meets the Atlantic Ocean. It was established in 1792. In addition to serving as a functioning navigational aid, it also serves as a memorial to the country's early nautical heritage.

Norfolk's Moses Myers House This city residence, constructed in the late 18th century, is a prime example of Federal-style architecture. It offers insights into the life of a wealthy early American family and previously belonged to Moses Myers, a well-known Jewish trader.

One of the earliest brick homes still standing in America is the Thoroughgood House in Virginia Beach, which has ties to Adam Thoroughgood, a significant early pioneer. Its design, which incorporates brickwork in English and Flemish bonds, harkens back to the popular architectural trends of Virginia in the 17th century.

Each historical site, with its bricks, beams, and shadows, has tales of aspiration, tenacity, creativity, and the human spirit. They act as concrete reminders of a past that paved the way for Norfolk and Virginia Beach's present and future, not merely as interesting areas of interest.

Chapter 5: Norfolk and Virginia Beach during the American Revolution

Indelible traces of the American Revolution, a pivotal time in the history of the country, may still be seen in Norfolk and Virginia Beach. As the struggle for independence from Britain grew more intense, these regions turned into hotbeds of ideological and military warfare.

Due to its advantageous location along the Elizabeth River, Norfolk became a center of the British economy. By the end of 1775, the situation had gotten out of hand, and the Battle of Great Bridge, a huge skirmish, was the result. In this battle, which took place just south of Norfolk, the Virginia militia defeated the British army, giving the colonies reason for celebration.

Norfolk's success was, however, fleeting. The final Royal Governor of Virginia, Lord Dunmore, led the British naval forces that reacted in January 1776. Following a ferocious bombardment, Norfolk, which was mainly regarded as a Loyalist town, was largely leveled. Because of how bad the destruction was, it took Norfolk several years to fully recover. Following this incident, Dunmore's defeat signaled the end of a large British military presence in Virginia, but the wounds from the battle persisted.

Due to its proximity to the Atlantic, Virginia Beach served as a prospective landing zone for British troops. Although there were no large-scale battles fought there, local militias were always on guard because to the looming threat. The region's waterways and shoreline were closely watched, and lookouts were placed to alert authorities to any signs of British expansion.

Beyond the physical clashes, the Revolution brought about societal and intellectual transformations. For instance, Norfolk's damage resulted in a fall in its Loyalist population. Those who supported the British Crown either retreated or maintained a low profile. Residents ardently supported the Continental Army and took part in Committees of Correspondence as a wave of Patriot zeal swept through.

The Revolution also affected the economy. Trade was impacted by the British blockade of American ports. Norfolk saw the effects because its port is one of its key sources of revenue. Smuggling spread as businesspeople looked for sneaky ways to transfer items in and out.

Africans who were held as slaves in Norfolk and Virginia Beach also encountered complicated circumstances. The British offered freedom to any slave who joined their forces in an effort to undermine the colonial economy and military endeavors. Many slaves left their plantations as a result of this declaration and joined the British in an effort to obtain freedom.

The scenery around Norfolk and Virginia Beach had undergone significant transformation by the time the Treaty of Paris was signed in 1783, officially bringing the Revolutionary War to an end. Battles, betrayals, sacrifices, and the unwavering spirit of a people determined to shape their own destiny had all been seen by them. Although the battle may have been over, these two great cities had just began their quest to rebuild and reinvent themselves in a new country.

Chapter 6: Local Heroes and Events of Note

Several local heroes emerged as the history of Norfolk and Virginia Beach was being woven, their deeds, choices, and bravery leaving enduring imprints on the history of the two towns. The historical legacy of the area has been influenced by these individuals and the significant occasions they were involved in, leaving tales of bravery, insight, and resiliency for future generations to tell.

John Ackiss must be brought up while talking about heroes. Ackiss was a well-known patriot who was born and raised in Princess Anne County, which is now Virginia Beach. His most significant deed occurred during the Revolutionary War when he gave crucial information to the colonial forces, which allowed them to repeatedly frustrate British intentions.

The "Witch of Pungo," Grace White Sherwood, was another notable individual. She was accused of witchcraft in the early 1700s, which was typical of the belief of the day. She famously participated in a "witch ducking" trial in Virginia Beach where she was shackled and thrown into the Lynnhaven River. She eventually was released after surviving this experience. She is now renowned for more than just the trial, including her tenacity and the wider discussion of discrimination in society.

Heroes from the Civil War emerged. Just west of Norfolk in Southampton County, William Mahone was a key player in the fight. He gained notoriety as a leading politician during the

Reconstruction era, fighting for the rights of the recently freed African Americans and was renowned for his tactical brilliance during the Battle of the Crater.

Heroes of a different kind emerged in the 20th century. Despite being from Norfolk, Joseph Jenkins Roberts is more known for his work abroad. He was elected as Liberia's first (and seventh) president, demonstrating the entwined history of the US and Liberia and Norfolk's covert participation therein.

Admiral Jeremy M. Boorda must be mentioned in any discussion of Norfolk heroes. He helped to shape contemporary naval plans while serving as the Chief of Naval Operations in the middle of the 1990s. Tragically, he passed away while serving, leaving a legacy of outstanding naval performance.

The history of the area is dotted with notable occasions. For instance, Virginia Beach was severely impacted by the 1933 Great Chesapeake Bay Hurricane. Because of the storm's impact on the coastline, Virginia Beach and Virginia's Eastern Shore are now connected via the Chesapeake Bay Bridge-Tunnel.

The Battle of Craney Island during the War of 1812 was another important occasion. In this combat, which took place close to Norfolk, American forces successfully repelled a British effort to capture the city; this win buoyed American spirits amid a war marked by ups and downs.

Numerous more heroes and occasions have also contributed to the rich tapestry of tales that Norfolk and Virginia Beach have to tell. They serve as symbols of the communities' tenacity, inventiveness, and spirit while resonating stories of success, tragedy, and hope.

Chapter 7: Post-Revolution Changes and Development

Following the American Revolution, Norfolk and Virginia Beach experienced a dramatic period as they navigated the intricacies of a young country looking for its identity and course.

Norfolk started down a road of renewal and reconstruction after sustaining significant damage during the war. The destruction caused by the British bombardment in 1776 left both a scar and an empty canvas. As trade sprang up again, Norfolk's beneficial port location became more and more clear. The city saw a rush of reconstruction work, and by the 1790s, brand-new brick buildings started to rise, signifying a rebirth from the ashes. The shoreline began to be lined by warehouses, business buildings, and townhouses.

Before, British laws had hindered trade, but now it was booming. One of the most important ports in the South, Norfolk's port, developed into a hive of activity. Exports of tobacco, cotton, and different agricultural products outweighed imports of European commodities, reestablishing the city's position as an important commercial hub for the fledgling country.

The economic upswing did not just affect Norfolk. Due to its closeness to both the Atlantic and the Chesapeake Bay, Virginia Beach experienced a boom in nautical activity. Shipping, oystering, and fishing all played major roles in the local economy. Additionally improving connectivity, roads and canals facilitated trade.

The post-Revolutionary age was a period of reflection and evolution for culture. The revolutionary ideals of the Enlightenment were increasingly influencing daily life. The region's focus shifted to education, resulting in the opening of schools and academies. The emergence of literary and debating organizations was a sign of a culture ready to engage in intellectual activities.

However, there were difficulties throughout this time as well. The institution of slavery, which was ingrained in Virginia's socioeconomic system, sparked heated discussion. While many people in the North started to support abolition, slavery continued to play a significant role in Virginia's economy, particularly its agriculture. This duality would lay the groundwork for conflicts that will explode in the next century.

Urban planning also received attention. The impact of the war's memory had taught people the value of city planning. In an effort to make Norfolk more resilient to potential future attacks or fires, streets were built out more methodically.

The area's agriculture underwent diversification. A more balanced agricultural economy resulted from farmers' post-Revolutionary experiments with crops like wheat and corn, which replaced the colonial era's primary crop of tobacco.

The post-American Revolutionary War years laid the groundwork for Norfolk and Virginia Beach. Cities embraced change, from the physical rebuilding of structures to the intellectual creation of society, laying the groundwork for the vibrant hubs of trade, culture, and community that they would become in the centuries that followed.

Chapter 8: Industry and Infrastructure Growth

In terms of industrial and infrastructure advancements, the late 18th and early 19th centuries were a pivotal time for Norfolk and Virginia Beach. As these areas started to play a significant role in the larger Southern economy, its pulsing heartbeat was felt strongly.

One of Norfolk's most valued assets in the past, the port, suffered considerable changes. Larger vessels may fit in the Elizabeth River's channels because to their extension and deepening. Due to its advantageous location on the mid-Atlantic coast, Norfolk developed into a key junction for both domestic and foreign trade lines. The invention of steamships at the beginning of the 19th century, which allowed for faster and more dependable transportation, helped to promote this commerce.

Another game-changer was the railroad's arrival in the middle of the 1800s. Norfolk had access to markets farther inland thanks to the Norfolk and Petersburg Railroad and later the Virginian Railway. These rail connections carried coal from the abundant mines of Western Virginia to the ports of Norfolk, where it was shipped all over the world.

On the other side, Virginia Beach experienced growth fueled by its abundant natural resources. The fishing business was boosted by the abundant waters of the Atlantic and Chesapeake Bay. Particularly oyster harvesting grew in importance as Virginia Beach oysters attained widespread acclaim.

Road infrastructure improvements helped both regions. Overland routes became more dependable and traveled faster because to the construction of macadamized roads. This not only made trading easier but also helped Virginia Beach become a more popular vacation spot, especially for people trying to get away from busy urban areas.

Banking and financial institutions became more necessary as trade and industries expanded. In order to meet this need and support the burgeoning business, Norfolk established a number of banks and financial institutions. Two organizations that were crucial during this time period were the Merchants and Farmers' Bank and the Bank of Virginia.

Trade and transportation were not the only areas of industrial progress. By the middle to end of the 19th century, Norfolk had seen the rise of numerous manufacturing companies. Along the city's landscape, textile factories, tobacco processing industries, and shipbuilding facilities sprang up. The late 18th-century Norfolk Naval Shipyard extended its operations and made a substantial contribution to the area's industrial character.

Despite the exponential rise of the industrial and infrastructure sectors, difficulties abounded. It was morally and ethically challenging for many of these sectors to depend on slave labor, especially in the early 19th century. The story was made more difficult by economic inequalities, environmental issues—particularly those related to overfishing—and the growing shadows of interstate strife before the Civil War.

However, despite these difficulties, Norfolk and Virginia Beach showed tenacity and a culture of entrepreneurship. Building blocks put down during this time helped shape the cities' trajectories and prepare them for the whirlwinds of the 20th century and beyond.

Chapter 9: Norfolk and Virginia Beach During the Civil War

The American Civil War, a turning point in history, had a significant impact on every region of the country. With their crucial geographic locations and intricate social structures, Norfolk and Virginia Beach were no exception. Their wartime experiences capture both the Civil War's overarching themes and particular regional dynamics.

Norfolk, the location of the Gosport Navy Yard (now known as the Norfolk Naval Shipyard), was immediately impacted by Virginia's choice to join the Confederacy at the start of the Civil War. Confederate forces, acting on orders from the governor of Virginia, set fire to the shipyard before Union forces could capture it despite their awareness of its significance. Large areas of the yard and numerous ships were destroyed in this act. The Confederacy did salvage one ship, the USS Merrimack, and turn it into the ironclad CSS Virginia. This ship later took part in the famous Battle of Hampton Roads against the USS Monitor of the Union, which was the first time two ironclad warships ever engaged in combat.

Although it seemed like most of the action was concentrated in Norfolk, Virginia Beach also had a part to play. Both Confederate and Union forces were interested in it because of its rivers and closeness to the Atlantic. The area saw clashes and was used by blockade runners seeking to evade Union naval patrols.

When Union forces led by Major General John E. Wool entered Norfolk in May 1862, it was a turning point for the city. General Benjamin Huger made the decision for the Confederates to leave with little opposition. This effectively secured the southern portion of the Chesapeake Bay for the remainder of the war and gave the Union a strategically important location. Union forces' control of Norfolk brought its own set of difficulties and dynamics. While some citizens left the city, others stayed and struggled to survive under military rule.

The conflict had significant societal and economic repercussions. Internal tensions grew in Norfolk, which had a mixed population of Union supporters and Confederate sympathizers. The city's economy, which was thriving prior to the war, suffered a great deal. Uncertainty was caused by trade restrictions, manufacturing disruptions, and occupation-related difficulties.

Local slaves had to contend with an environment that was changing as well. Many people saw the oncoming Union forces as a sign of independence. Some slaves took the initiative and escaped, seeking safety with Union forces. They frequently found employment supporting the army or navy as workers or even as enlisted men in organizations like the United States Colored Troops.

Both Norfolk and Virginia Beach experienced the effects of the war, including a landscape scarred by warfare, a community coping with the abolition of slavery, and the difficulty of Reconstruction. Families grieved the loss of loved ones, buildings bore the scars of the war, and the entire region was left to consider the ramifications of a united but drastically altered country.

In Norfolk and Virginia Beach, the Civil War left a legacy of tenacity in the face of change. From the skirmishes and naval engagements to the experiences of common people, the tales from this time period provide a microcosm of the larger American experience during its most trying time.

Chapter 10: Reconstruction and its Impact

The United States was still experiencing turmoil after the Civil War ended. From 1865 through 1877, a time of rebuilding, realignment, and redefinition was known as the Reconstruction era. Given their strategic importance during the war and their diverse demographics, Norfolk and Virginia Beach were highlighted in the post-war American narrative.

In the immediate aftermath of the war, Norfolk was in ruins, its formerly bustling port was failing, and many of its structures bore the signs of battle. However, a surge of federal investments and efforts to repair the city's infrastructure occurred during the Reconstruction era. Restoring the Norfolk Naval Shipyard's status as an important naval base was of particular significance.

Virginia Beach, which is less urbanized than Norfolk, encountered difficulties stemming more from changes to its socioeconomic structure than from physical reconstruction. Its traditional agrarian economy, which primarily relied on the institution of slavery, needed to be redesigned. Sharecropping and tenant farming, where freedmen and poor whites would labor the land and provide the landowners a percentage of their harvests as rent, were born out of this shift.

Civil rights were redefined during the Reconstruction, which was one of the most significant changes. The 13th, 14th, and 15th Amendments were ratified in an effort to eliminate slavery, extend citizenship to everyone born in the United States, and guarantee the right to vote for all male citizens, regardless of color. Following these modifications, Norfolk had a growth in African American neighborhoods, congregations, and businesses. In order to educate the newly emancipated populace, freedmen's schools were constructed.

These developments, though, were not without opposition. The emergence of white supremacist organizations and the adoption of "Black Codes" aimed to limit and erode African Americans' rights. Like many southern regions, Norfolk and Virginia Beach experienced racial and political problems. The turbulent political scene saw a swing between conservative Democrats who wanted to reinstate pre-war racial hierarchies and radical Republicans who wanted to guarantee rights for African Americans.

The area's economy started to diversify. Although agriculture, notably the production of cotton and peanuts, continued to be significant, there was a clear shift towards more diverse sectors. The port of Norfolk started operating again, gradually regaining its liveliness from before the war. The expansion of railroads, particularly the Norfolk and Western Railway's extension, contributed to the area's economic resurgence.

However, the federal forces were withdrawn with the conclusion of Reconstruction in 1877, which resulted in a decrease in the implementation of civil rights laws. This paved the way for the advent of the Jim Crow era, which presented significant difficulties for the African American communities in Norfolk and Virginia Beach.

In Norfolk and Virginia Beach, the Reconstruction era was essentially a time of promise, development, and substantial difficulties. This era was one of the most dynamic and significant in the history of the area because of the tension between advancement and opposition, between the ideals of equality and the realities of bigotry.

Chapter 11: Norfolk and Virginia Beach in the Gilded Age

The Gilded Age, usually defined as the time span from the 1870s to the 1900s, was marked by a rapid industrialization, enormous wealth accumulation, and sharp socioeconomic inequities. This period was characterized by expansion, diversification, and the introduction of fresh sociocultural dynamics in Norfolk and Virginia Beach.

The port's significance increased dramatically in Norfolk. The flow of commodities through its docks grew constant with the development of steamships and an increasingly integrated global economy. As a center for the commerce in cotton, peanuts, and tobacco, the city attracted traders from both domestic and foreign markets. In close proximity to this, the seafood sector saw a boom, particularly in the export of oysters and crab. Due to the resulting affluence, impressive structures, opulent homes, and elaborate public places were built, which served as a reflection of the era's prosperity.

Railroad expansion remained an important growth-promoting factor. By expanding its network, the Norfolk and Western Railway made it easier for coal from Appalachian mines to be exported. This improved Norfolk's economic standing and also sped up urbanization and the growth of areas near railway crossings.

In the meantime, Virginia Beach started to change from a largely agricultural setting to a developing tourist destination.

Residents from neighboring cities now have easy access to the area's magnificent beaches and tranquil surroundings because to the completion of the Norfolk and Virginia Beach Railroad in the late 19th century. Although its foundations were laid during the Gilded Age, this reputation would eventually be cemented with the erection of the opulent Cavalier Hotel in 1927.

But despite its glittering appearance of affluence, the Gilded Age was marked by glaring inequality. Due to the concentration of wealth among industrialists and traders, socioeconomic divisions resulted. In Norfolk, labor movements started to pick up steam, particularly among dock workers and those employed in the expanding industrial industries. They demanded higher pay, better working conditions, and flexible hours.

The end of Reconstruction and the beginning of the Jim Crow era meant systemic racial discrimination, segregation, and disenfranchisement for the African American communities in both regions. Despite this hardship, Black Norfolk churches, businesses, and social groups grew, strengthening local ties and promoting civil rights.

A cultural renaissance was also experienced throughout the Gilded Age. With a burgeoning urban population, Norfolk saw the emergence of theaters, opera houses, and amusement establishments. Literature, the arts, and music started to capture the grandeur and undercurrents of the time. Virginia Beach attracted a more bohemian crowd as a result of its beautiful beauty inspiring artists and authors.

Both Norfolk and Virginia Beach had changed dramatically from their post-Civil War personalities by the turn of the century. They served as miniature representations of the Gilded Age in America as a whole, glistening with gold on the outside but hiding complexity and difficulties on the inside.

Chapter 12: The Rise of Technology and its Effects

As America entered the 20th century, technological developments started to have a significant impact on the country's societal structure, economy, and way of life. With their distinct geographies and socioeconomic systems, Norfolk and Virginia Beach were in a position to closely observe and interact with these changes.

The development of transportation and logistics immediately benefited Norfolk, which has a thriving port and expanding industrial base. The port's adoption of motorized cranes and cutting-edge cargo handling technologies allowed for the rapid loading and unloading of cargo, increasing trade productivity. The city's tram lines were also electrified, which sped up daily journeys and seamlessly connected different areas of Norfolk.

Businesses in Norfolk found themselves connected to a fast contracting world with the invention of the telegraph and, later, the telephone. Now, transactions that used to take days or weeks can be completed in a matter of hours. For traders and businesspeople who needed real-time information to make judgments, this was very helpful.

Technology has been used by Virginia Beach's newly developing tourism industry. Hotels started to brag about having electric lighting, telephone connections, and even rudimentary air conditioning. These contemporary conveniences, which were considered luxuries at the time, drew a wealthier clientele and cemented Virginia Beach's status as a premier vacation destination.

The advancement of technology also affected the agriculture industry. The development of farming tools like tractors and motorized plows allowed for the less labor-intensive cultivation of wider areas of land. In addition to increasing yields, this signaled the start of the transition from labor-intensive farming to increasingly mechanized agriculture.

The rapid development of technology wasn't without problems, though. The working class in Norfolk got increasingly uneasy as industries there became more mechanized. In many cases, machines started to take the place of physical labor, which sparked worker unrest and calls for increased job security. These technological shocks can be partly blamed for the emergence of labor unions during this time.

The African American communities in Norfolk and Virginia Beach had new channels for organizing and communication because to technology. Radio and print media's increased reach meant that voices promoting social justice and civil rights could reach a larger audience. Organizations used these platforms to mobilize support, spread knowledge, and challenge the pervasive racial prejudices of the time.

Concerns about pollution and the depletion of natural resources were raised as a result of Norfolk's industrial expansion, which was fueled by technical improvements. The city's rivers, which are crucial to its identity and economy, were threatened by industrial effluents and required protection.

It was evident by the first half of the 20th century that technology was not simply a driver for change but also a cornerstone of the time. It posed a patchwork of potential and difficulties for Norfolk and Virginia Beach, a force that might help them enter a new era of prosperity but also one that needed to be carefully managed to protect the safety of all of its citizens.

Chapter 13: Norfolk and Virginia Beach during WWI and WWII

The United States' participation in both World Wars I and II had a significant impact on its cities and towns, including Norfolk and Virginia Beach. These conflicts were turning points in world history. The socio-economic and cultural landscapes of these regions were shaped by the geopolitical repercussions of these wars as well as their immediate effects.

Due to its key naval facilities, Norfolk had a significant role in the start of World War I. One of the biggest naval shipyards in the world, Norfolk Naval Shipyard, increased production and concentrated on providing shipbuilding and repair services to support the American war effort. Thousands of people flocked to the city in search of work, which caused a population boom and a parallel increase in housing and infrastructure.

Despite having less industry than Norfolk, Virginia Beach was still affected by the Great War. German U-boats raised worries that the shoreline should be closely monitored, which led to the construction of lookout posts and coastal defenses.

The socio-cultural fabric was subject to a significant impact from WWI as well. Women entered the labor in greater numbers, disrupting traditional gender roles, as males left for the European front. Additionally, the war served as a stimulus for the Great Migration, which saw a large number of African Americans leave the rural South for urban areas like Norfolk in search of better job prospects and to avoid racial violence.

World War II: Norfolk's significance in the American naval strategy had only increased by the time World War II broke out. The Norfolk Naval Base, established during the interwar years, grew to be the biggest in the world and played a crucial role in both the war's Atlantic and Pacific theaters. Naval operations, training, and logistics centralized at Norfolk.

Once more, the shipyard was a hive of activity, this time with an emphasis on the construction of battleships, aircraft carriers, and other essential navy vessels. The need for speed in the war effort hastened technological developments and advances in weapons and ship design.

Due to its proximity to Norfolk, Virginia Beach was affected by these military operations inadvertently. Businesses in Virginia Beach, particularly those involved in hospitality and entertainment, prospered as a result of the consistent influx of military personnel and their families. Additionally, Virginia Beach's Fort Story developed into a crucial coastal defense artillery training center.

The conflict did, however, also bring with it some difficulties. Housing constraints and infrastructure strain resulted from the shipyard and naval base's population expansion in Norfolk. Rationing and blackouts became commonplace, affecting daily life. Nevertheless, there was a strong sense of solidarity among the people, who participated in war bond campaigns, volunteered for civil defense, and gave money to the men fighting abroad.

WWII was a time of ironies for the African American communities in both cities. While many bravely fought for democracy in segregated units abroad, they returned home to prejudice and discrimination. The Civil Rights Movement, however, also saw its beginnings during the war years, since there were more cries for racial justice and equality.

After World War II, a lot of things changed. A period of readjustment followed the return of the military personnel. The G.I. Bill changed the socioeconomic dynamics of Norfolk and Virginia Beach by enabling many people to pursue college and homeownership.

To sum up, the World Wars affected Norfolk and Virginia Beach in more ways than merely as distant geopolitical events. major were pivotal eras that altered the economic, social, and cultural environments of major towns and permanently altered their histories.

Chapter 14: Military Bases and Economics During WWII

The American military's presence in Norfolk and Virginia Beach during World War II grew to have a powerful influence on the region's economy, social, and physical environment. These cities, which were strategically located along the Atlantic coast, were crucial to naval and ground operations.

During World War II, Naval Station Norfolk developed into a key node for the American Navy. By the middle of the war, this base, which is located along the Chesapeake Bay's borders, was the biggest naval station in the entire world. From the deployment of the Atlantic Fleet operations to comprehensive training programs for sailors, this complex handled a wide range of missions. Tens of thousands of navy men arrived, bringing with them a significant boost to the local economy. As they served to these service members and their families, local businesses, from eateries to clothing stores, saw a boom.

The Norfolk Naval Shipyard in Portsmouth increased the scope of its operations across the Elizabeth River from Norfolk. The shipyard, which is renowned for its ability to build and repair ships, went into overdrive, producing and maintaining a large number of battleships important for the Atlantic and Pacific theaters. This activity required a sizable workforce and attracted workers from all over the nation, which increased the population and sparked a housing boom at the same time.

Despite being smaller than the naval behemoths at Norfolk, Virginia Beach's Fort Story had a special place in the wider war machine. Before the war, its main purpose was to train coastal artillery, but as the war progressed, its operations varied and grew more intense, concentrating on preparing men for amphibious assaults, a strategy that would become crucial in operations like D-Day.

The effects of this military buildup on the economy were extensive. To accommodate the expanding population, real estate developers hurried to build homes, apartments, and facilities. Prices for goods and services in the area skyrocketed due to the sudden increase in demand. A level of urban growth never before witnessed in the area was sparked by the growing population.

However, it went beyond only housing and shopping. The area's industrial structure was likewise altered by the military bases' presence. Many auxiliary industries emerged, from food processing facilities serving the bases to companies making ship and airplane parts. Norfolk's port facilities grew and were updated to meet the needs of both commercial and military vessels.

Despite the expansion of the economy, the war presented several difficulties. Resources were depleted as a result of the intense demand from both the military and the civilian sectors. Due to shortages of goods like rubber, gasoline, and some groceries, rationing became a way of life. Public utilities and services are also under pressure as a result of the increased urbanization and immigration.

Beyond its immediate economic effects, WWII's military presence altered the socio-cultural environment. Women began to fill roles that had historically been filled by men when men left the country, particularly in shipyards and industries. This change started to quietly change ideas about the roles and skills of women and men. The time of the war was a mixed blessing for the African American community. While many of them were able to secure employment in the expanding defense sectors, they were nevertheless forced to deal with systematic racism and segregation.

It was clear that Norfolk and Virginia Beach had undergone an irreversible transformation at the end of World War II. These communities had been redefined by the military bases, which had a significant economic impact and put them on a different course for the ensuing decades.

Chapter 15: Norfolk and Virginia Beach in the Civil Rights Era

The struggle for racial equality typified the turbulent Civil Rights Era, which spanned the middle of the 20th century. As a part of the larger South, Norfolk and Virginia Beach were intricately woven into this complicated web of social change, resistance, and final transformation.

African Americans in both cities, many of whom had bravely served in the war, started to demand an end to the institutionalized racial segregation and discrimination that had long been a part of their life following World War II. A number of significant national events, including the historic Supreme Court ruling in Brown v. Board of Education in 1954 that declared racial segregation in public schools unconstitutional, helped to fuel this newly found momentum.

However, the choice did not immediately result in desegregation. Instead, it encountered strong opposition in Norfolk. The mayor and a sizable percentage of the white population in the city looked for ways to get around the decision. When the city decided to close six of its public schools rather than integrate them, this defiance came to a head in 1958. During this occasion, known as the "Massive Resistance," white state authorities, especially those in Norfolk, vehemently opposed desegregation measures. For several months, the schools were shuttered, disrupting education and bringing racial tensions to the fore.

Though less overt than in Norfolk, there was still a noticeable opposition to accepting integration among many white citizens of Virginia Beach. African Americans were frequently confined to underfunded and badly maintained areas in Virginia Beach's public facilities, including beaches and recreational areas.

The African American community in both places stayed steadfast in the face of challenges. Churches were crucial in the civil rights movement because they not only served as places of worship but also as gathering sites for activists to plan actions. Local leaders emerged to lead the battle for equality as grass-roots groups took shape. Demonstrations, sit-ins, and boycotts increased in frequency as a result of the injustice, which inspired support.

The tide started to turn as the 1960s went on. Both the Voting Rights Act of 1965 and the Civil Rights Act of 1964 were significant pieces of federal legislation that established the legal foundation for challenging and dismantling long-standing racial segregation and discrimination systems. Schools in Norfolk and Virginia Beach were finally desegregated by the late 1960s and early 1970s, while difficulties persisted in assuring balanced resources and opportunities for children from all backgrounds.

Both cities had an increase in African American political representation during this time period. After voting restrictions were eliminated, African Americans started to win elections for municipal offices, gradually altering the political climate and ensuring that their opinions and concerns were considered when making decisions about the city.

Although there was a lot of conflict throughout the Civil Rights Era, there was also a lot of change and tremendous resiliency. Together with national movements, the African American communities in Norfolk and Virginia Beach worked to radically alter the social, cultural, and political landscape of these cities, paving the way for a more inclusive future.

Chapter 16: Other Notable Social Movements in Norfolk and Virginia Beach

Throughout the 20th century, Norfolk and Virginia Beach served as hubs of active activism and societal change outside of the historic Civil Rights Movement. These cities gave their particular contributions while bearing witness to the larger changes in the country, from the breezes of feminism to the roars against war.

By the middle of the century, feminism was starting to take root in the area as a result of the women's suffrage campaign, which reached its height in 1920. Organizations like the Virginia Beach Women's Club contributed to community giving as well as advocacy for women's social, economic, and educational rights. Women in Norfolk and Virginia Beach organized grassroots initiatives addressing problems like pay inequity and reproductive rights as the feminism wave of the 1960s and 1970s swept the nation. Colleges and universities evolved into forums where male and female students discussed these urgent issues, creating the foundation for alterations in regional policies and mindsets.

Another type of societal unrest was brought to the region by the Vietnam War. Many families in Norfolk and Virginia Beach had direct connections to the overseas battle due to their strong military infrastructure. Anti-war sentiment increased as the war continued on, especially among the younger residents. Rallies and protests in favor of and against the war were frequent occurrences. Peaceful protests, vigils, and occasionally physical altercations between pro- and anti-war demonstrators may be seen on Norfolk's streets.

Environmentalism left its effect as well. Local organizations fought for tighter environmental safeguards as awareness of pollution in the Chesapeake Bay and the Atlantic Ocean expanded. By the late 1970s and early 1980s, cleanup efforts, marine ecosystem education campaigns, and protests against industrial pollution had become commonplace. The cities' adoption of sustainability programs during the next decades was made possible by this environmental consciousness.

In the latter half of the 20th century, the region responded to the national appeal for acceptance and equality by supporting the LGBTQ+ rights movement. Even in the early stages of the AIDS crisis, grassroots organizations and advocacy groups arose despite initial opposition. Events like PrideFest helped Norfolk's LGBTQ+ community flourish throughout time by celebrating diversity and spreading acceptance.

Last but not least, as public awareness of disabilities and the rights of people with disabilities rose, so did regional movements calling for improved facilities, care, and societal acceptance. There were groups formed that worked to increase accessibility, provide resources, and guarantee that people with disabilities may live happy, meaningful lives.

Together, these movements enhanced Norfolk and Virginia Beach's social fabric. Even while each wave of action had a different goal in mind, they all shared the desire for a more accepting, compassionate, and equal society.

Chapter 17: Technological Revolution of the 20th Century to the Millennium

As the 20th century drew near, a wave of technical advancements was about to sweep the globe, reshaping every aspect of daily life, the economy, and society. With their advantageous locations and diversified populations, Norfolk and Virginia Beach were not just bystanders but engaged participants in this transformation.

The importance of these two towns as maritime hubs played a critical role in embracing and advancing technological innovations at the onset. Some of the biggest shipyards on the East Coast, those in Norfolk, adopted contemporary technologies swiftly. The shipyards served as an example of how traditional sectors may change in response to technological advancement, from more effective shipbuilding techniques through the introduction of electronic navigation systems in the second part of the twentieth century.

The invention of the automobile altered city planning and transportation in both cities. In the early to mid-20th century, as cars became more affordable to the average American, roads, highways, and bridges grew and changed. In addition to connecting Virginia's Eastern Shore to Virginia Beach, the 1964 construction of the Chesapeake Bay Bridge-Tunnel was a marvel of its day and served as a showcase for engineering advancements of the time.

The spread of telecommunications technologies after World War II became obvious. Telephone networks crisscrossed communities, connecting people and companies in ways that had never been possible. Early adopters in Norfolk and Virginia Beach were the schools and companies as computers started to become commonplace in the 1980s. Computer science courses have been introduced, and Virginia Beach colleges and Old Dominion University in Norfolk have started incorporating computer-based learning into their curricula.

The environment of the media was not unaffected. Early 20th-century radio stations altered entertainment and news distribution, followed by television transmissions in the second half of the century. Pioneering stations like WTKR-TV in Norfolk gave locals a fresh perspective on the world and influenced local culture.

The development of the internet and cellular technology in the 1990s highlighted the progression of this revolution. In order to bridge the digital divide as much as possible, public libraries in both cities were crucial in giving locals their first online encounters. Local firms quickly adapted, adopting online platforms and digital technologies to stay competitive in an industry that was quickly going global.

An economic lifeline, the port of Norfolk, also underwent changes. Logistics were transformed by automated methods for processing cargo, computerized shipment tracking, and integrated communication platforms, ensuring that the port remained one of the most effective and technologically cutting-edge in the nation.

By the time the new millennium arrived, Norfolk and Virginia Beach were not just witnesses to the technological revolution but also bright canvases on which it had been painted. The changes brought about by this time period affected residents' ways of working, playing, communicating, and seeing the future on a deeply sociological level as well as in terms of infrastructure.

Chapter 18: Changing Demographics and Culture of the 20th Century to the Millennium

For Norfolk and Virginia Beach, the 20th century saw quick and major demographic changes, which were accompanied by a fundamental transformation in cultural norms, values, and culture. Both communities were healing from the socioeconomic wounds of the Civil War and Reconstruction at the turn of the century, as was much of the South. However, as the years went by, they would see astonishing changes firsthand and take part in them.

Migration Trends: During the early to mid-20th century's Great Migration, many African Americans relocated from the rural South to the urban North in search of better employment prospects and to escape the oppressive Jim Crow laws. Numerous people relocated to urban centers like Norfolk, but a sizeable portion also did so, bringing with them new cultural influences, music, food, and traditions.

Parallel to the two World Wars, a variety of immigrants from around the nation were drawn to both cities by the economic opportunities offered by the marine and military sectors. Veterans who decided to live in the area after World War II were drawn by the area's promise of stability and the allure of beach living.

Diverse Communities: By the middle of the 20th century, international immigrants started to swell in Norfolk and

Virginia Beach. Due to their connections to the navy, Filipino communities developed themselves and brought with them unique cultural, culinary, and religious practices. People from Latin America, South Asia, the Middle East, and other regions of the world started to call these cities home later in the century as globalization took root, enhancing the local tapestry with a variety of languages, festivals, and traditions.

Cultural Renaissance: These population changes sparked cultural advancements. Jazz, blues, gospel, and later rock, soul, and hip-hop found ardent supporters and practitioners in the region as music experienced dramatic changes. Too many different food options. As the population became more diverse, new restaurants arose, serving meals from the Philippines, Latin America, India, and the Middle East alongside the staples of seafood and traditional Southern cuisine.

Values Change: As the century went on, societal values underwent subtle but significant changes. Both cities were significantly impacted by the Civil Rights Movement of the 1960s, which resulted in more racial integration, the repeal of Jim Crow laws, and a stronger focus on equality. In the latter half of the century, movements for LGBTQ+ rights, environmental awareness, and women's liberation all added to the challenge and expansion of social standards.

As the 20th century came to a close, Norfolk and Virginia Beach's population composition had significantly changed from when it had started. The cities had developed into mingles of customs, ideals, and civilizations. Both towns were prepared to meet the opportunities and challenges of the 21st century with a diversified and energetic population thanks to this rich mosaic, which would serve as the foundation for the new millennium.

Chapter 19: Post-9/11 Norfolk and Virginia Beach

The September 11, 2001 terrorist attacks marked a turning point for the United States and sent shockwaves even to areas far from Ground Zero. With their strategic military importance and coastal locations, Norfolk and Virginia Beach were among the places that underwent significant changes in the aftermath.

Enhancements to Security: Immediately after the attacks, security precautions were significantly increased. Security procedures increased dramatically in Norfolk, which is home to military Station Norfolk, the largest military installation in the world. Access to the base grew more limited, and severe inspections became the norm. Both cities' waterfronts experienced increased patrols and observation. There was increased monitoring of bridges, tunnels, and other crucial infrastructure points, including the Chesapeake Bay Bridge-Tunnel.

Economic Impact: Uncertainty characterized the early economic aftermath. People were reluctant to travel, which negatively impacted Virginia Beach's tourism industry, a major source of income. However, federal defense spending rose in the years that followed, and Norfolk, which is home to a lot of military infrastructure, saw a surge in related economic activity.

One of the wonderful effects of this awful time was the collective resilience and camaraderie displayed by the citizens of both cities. Vigils, community get-togethers, and memorial services as well as deeds of kindness, humanitarian endeavors, and volunteer efforts intended to aid first responders, afflicted families, and deployed military became common sights. Schools, religious organizations, and community centers were crucial in providing citizens with counseling and support as they dealt with the emotional fallout.

Military Deployments: As the United States entered the Afghanistan and Iraq conflicts, there was a rise in military deployments to Norfolk and Virginia Beach due to their strategic importance. Families said heartfelt goodbyes to their service members, and local support networks were strengthened to help those left behind. Cities developed into gathering places for farewells and homecomings, and tales of bravery, selflessness, and tenacity were woven into the local lore.

Cultural Shifts: The 9/11 attacks caused a change in cultural viewpoints and beliefs. There was a rise in curiosity about world issues, civilizations, and religions, especially Islam. However, this time period also saw instances of mistrust and prejudice toward particular communities, highlighting the difficult issues society faced.

Initiatives for Preparedness: The 9/11 attacks highlighted the significance of being ready. Both communities made major investments in community education, disaster preparedness exercises, and emergency response training. More than ever, the significance of first responders was emphasized, and funds were spent to guarantee that they had the best gear and training available.

Unquestionably, the way of life in Norfolk and Virginia Beach changed in the years after 9/11. While the horrific events of that day remained in the background, they also served to emphasize the communities' resiliency, cohesion, and strength. Both towns navigated the challenges of a new world while hoping for a better future during the post-9/11 era, which was characterized by a mix of vigilance and hope.

Chapter 20: Contemporary Challenges and Opportunities

The problems and opportunities that Norfolk and Virginia Beach encountered as they entered the twenty-first century were distinct and influenced by their respective histories, geographical settings, and socioeconomic dynamics.

Environmental and coastline Challenges: The prospect of rising sea levels and coastline erosion has been one of the most important issues for both cities. They are particularly sensitive to the effects of climate change since they are located near the Atlantic coast and the Chesapeake Bay. Concerns regarding the viability and habitability of some places have been raised by the frequent floods, especially in sections of Norfolk. Hurricanes and storm surges have occasionally caused devastation, highlighting the need for creative approaches to coastal management.

Economic Diversification: Although the military and maritime sectors have historically been important to both towns, there has been an effort to broaden the economy. The governmental and private sectors have invested in the fields of technology, healthcare, tourism, and renewable energy, increasing the opportunities in these fields.

Infrastructure Development: Given the cities' rapid growth and the deterioration of existing facilities, transportation and infrastructure have remained a challenge. The focus has been on modernizing public transportation, strengthening road systems, and developing digital infrastructure. To address environmental issues, there has also been a strong focus in creating sustainable infrastructure.

Cultural and demographic shifts: With the population's shifting demographics, it has become more important than ever to ensure inclusivity and meet the wide range of requirements of the populace. This includes opportunity for newcomers to integrate into the community, access to services in several languages, and healthcare that is sensitive to cultural differences.

Housing and urban development have been major concerns, as they have been in many other urban areas across the nation. The needs of expanding populations have to be balanced with sustainable urban development, community preservation, and historical significance.

Education and Workforce Training: With the change to a more technologically advanced world, it has become increasingly important to guarantee that the local workforce has the necessary skills. It has been vital to make investments in STEM (Science, Technology, Engineering, and Mathematics) education, career training, and higher education institutions.

Tourism and branding: Both cities have acknowledged that tourism has the potential to be a big economic force. They have been marketed as must-see locations by emphasizing their historic history, stunning seaside scenery, and vibrant culture.

Both communities have had to adapt and innovate in their public health and safety policies in response to issues including the opioid crisis, mental health issues, and changing public safety needs.

The resiliency and flexibility of Norfolk and Virginia Beach have stood out in the face of the many difficulties. They continue to carve out their stories while embracing the chances presented by a world that is changing quickly and aiming for a harmonious balance between growth and preservation.

Chapter 21: Famous Personalities from Norfolk and Virginia Beach

Numerous noteworthy individuals from a variety of areas have come from or called Norfolk and Virginia Beach home. Each of these individuals has had an enduring impression on society at large.

Music:

Pharrell Williams is a well-known singer, songwriter, producer, and fashion designer who is from Virginia Beach. His influence extends beyond music into broader cultural spheres. He is known for his particular style and singles like "Happy".

Missy Elliott is a local legend in the music business who was born and raised in Portsmouth before relocating to Virginia Beach. She is a multiple Grammy Award-winning rapper, singer, songwriter, and record producer who has created a number of top singles for the public.

Timbaland, real name Timothy Mosley, is a well-known music producer, rapper, and songwriter who was born in Norfolk. He is renowned for his distinctive and avant-garde sound and has worked with some of the biggest names in music.

Terrence Thornton, better known by his stage name Pusha T, is a rapper and record executive from Virginia Beach who is another musical prodigy.

Sports:

Bruce Smith is a retired American football defensive end who predominantly played for the Buffalo Bills in the NFL. He was born in Norfolk. He is recognized as one of the best defensive ends and is a member of the Hall of Fame.

Gabby Douglas: This Olympic gold medallist called Virginia Beach home. In 2012, Gabby made history by becoming the first African American woman to win the individual all-around gold medal at the Olympics.

Alonzo Mourning is a former NBA player and Olympic gold winner best known for his time with the Miami Heat. Mourning was born in Chesapeake, a city close to Norfolk and Virginia Beach.

Ryan Zimmerman was up in Virginia Beach but was born in Washington, North Carolina and has played for the Washington Nationals his whole Major League Baseball career.

Journalism and literary works:

Margaret Sullavan was born in Norfolk and became a well-known actress and star of classic Hollywood movies including "The Shop Around the Corner."

Wiley Cash: Although he wasn't born in either place, this renowned author spent significant time in Virginia Beach where he drew inspiration from the people and tales there.

V.C. Andrews: The well-known writer of the "Flowers in the Attic" series was born in Portsmouth and lived in Norfolk for a sizable portion of her life.

Will Harris is a well-known journalist from Virginia Beach who has contributed to numerous prestigious magazines. Harris has written extensively about television, pop culture, and music.

Film and television:

Grant Aleksander: The actor who won an Emmy nomination for his performance in the venerable soap opera "Guiding Light" was born in Norfolk.

Known for his flawless celebrity impersonations on "Saturday Night Live," actor and comedian Jay Pharoah is from Chesapeake and has lived in Virginia Beach for a sizable portion of his life.

Politics and the military:

Douglas MacArthur, a general, was born in Little Rock, Arkansas, and later moved to Norfolk. The Douglas MacArthur Memorial, a museum and archive devoted to his life and achievements, was created by the city as a mark of respect for him.

Business and charitable giving:

Frank Batten, a well-known philanthropist and founder of the Weather Channel, was born in Norfolk. He has made significant contributions to the media industry, and his charitable work will live on in perpetuity.

Health and Science:

Roger L. Easton: Easton lived and worked in Virginia Beach after being born in Craftsbury, Vermont. His achievements, as a key player in the creation of the GPS (Global Positioning System), had a long-lasting effect on the entire world.

Each of these people has been shaped by the vibrant cultures, difficulties, and possibilities of Norfolk and Virginia Beach in their own special ways. They serve as examples of the cities' capacity to develop talent, stimulate greatness, and have a wide range of global impacts.

Chapter 22: Norfolk and Virginia Beach as Seen on TV

In both cameo and starring parts, Norfolk and Virginia Beach have frequently been the focus of the bright lights of television. These locations are frequently used as backdrops and subjects for numerous television programs due to their maritime significance, visual beauty, and particular regional culture. Let's examine how these two cities have been portrayed on television in more detail.

Crime Dramas & Military Shows

It makes sense that military-themed shows would be interested in Norfolk's significant naval presence. even though it wasn't strictly filmed there:

The U.S. Navy-focused legal drama "JAG" has periodically based one of its episodes on an incident that occurred at the Norfolk naval facility. The plotlines of the show have emphasized the tactical importance of Norfolk's naval activities.

Episodes of "NCIS" have occasionally included a naval setting because of the show's focus on military crimes.

Real-time TV

Both cities have appeared in reality TV programs, notably those that focus on food, travel, or treasure hunting, in addition to being the setting for fictional depictions.

A visit to the "Beach Pub" by "Diners, Drive-ins, and Dives" highlighted Virginia Beach's seafood sector by showcasing its mouthwatering crab cakes and fresh flounder.

In Virginia Beach, the "Antiques Roadshow" held one of their appraisal sessions, sharing local gems and tales.

Documentaries

Both cities have beautiful natural settings and extensive historical archives, making them popular topics for documentaries.

Norfolk is shown in "World War II in HD" in order to highlight the strategic importance of the city during the conflict.

In its examination of the Atlantic Flyway, "Nature" included Virginia Beach, emphasizing the migrating birds and the city's distinctive coastal habitat.

Sitcoms and Daytime Television: Although less frequently, Norfolk and Virginia Beach have been mentioned in sitcoms and daytime television shows.

A character named Holt Richter in "The Cleveland Show" makes the passing reference that he is from Virginia Beach.

The scenic setting served as the setting for several parts of a special summer episode of "The Today Show" that was recorded in Virginia Beach.

Local programming: Local television is essential for capturing the real pulse of the area.

A lifestyle program called "The Hampton Roads Show" does an excellent job of capturing the spirit of Norfolk, Virginia Beach, and the places around them by featuring local tales, highlighting upcoming events, and showcasing local artists.

Popular locations for filming

The following locations are increasingly popular with television crews:

The gorgeous Virginia Beach Boardwalk, which offers sweeping vistas of the Atlantic Ocean, has been highlighted in a number of travel and lifestyle shows.

The NEON District in Norfolk, which is well-known for its colorful murals, has served as the setting for programs and segments about art.

The Battleship and Nauticus Wisconsin: Because of its naval heritage, it has been featured in historical and naval warfare-related documentaries.

Through these particular programs and locations, Norfolk and Virginia Beach have had their tales told to audiences across the country and around the world, exhibiting the area's distinctive fusion of history, culture, and natural beauty.

Chapter 23: Norfolk and Virginia Beach as Depicted in Literature

With its vastness and boundless possibilities, literature frequently more profoundly conveys the spirit of a location than any snapshot or video could. Authors and poets have evoked the character, nuances, and spirit of Norfolk and Virginia Beach through the printed word. Here is a tour of some of the notable authors and literary works that have included these cities into the vocabulary of literature:

Mary Helen Washington's book Willie Mae, which is set in Norfolk during World War II, depicts a city that is coping with racial tensions and the effects of war. The story centers on a young black woman, providing readers with an insightful look at racial dynamics and the complexities of life at the time.

David Baldacci: A well-known thriller and crime author from Virginia, Baldacci occasionally uses Virginia Beach as the setting for his convoluted stories, lending the setting more credibility to his tense narratives.

The book "The Blood of Emmett Till" by Timothy B. Tyson: Although this work isn't specifically about Norfolk or Virginia Beach, it nevertheless has meaningful ties. The harrowing narrative of Emmett Till is intricately entwined with Virginia's own racial history. The region's responses to the Till case and references to it help to illustrate the historical racial dynamics at work.

The Wettest & The Driest: Vee Spare's illustration perfectly illustrates the contrast of Virginia Beach's natural surroundings. The author conjures a clear picture of the surroundings, from its swampy wetlands to its sun-baked boardwalks, through poetic words.

Local anthologies: Norfolk and Virginia Beach frequently appear in the annual "Hampton Roads Writers Anthology" of literary works. These volumes of writings comprise poems, short stories, and essays that discuss local culture and the diverse experiences of its people.

By Raymond L. Harper, author of "Norfolk & Virginia Beach: A Pictorial History": Despite being essentially a photographic record, Harper's in-depth descriptions and supplementary text offer a thorough exploration of the region's rich history. The narrative weaves a literary and visual portrait of the area from its first settlers to the present.

The locations in Ellery Adams' mystery series are fictional, yet they strikingly resemble the Virginia Beach and Norfolk region, and Adams has acknowledged that the Hampton Roads region serves as inspiration.

Poetry: Many poets have been influenced by the distinctive beauty of Norfolk and Virginia Beach. Virginia's shoreline is mentioned in anthologies like "Poetry of the American South," recalling the distinctive sights, sounds, and emotions of the area.

William Wilkinson's "Waterways to the World": This book, which is centered on the port city of Norfolk, blends together history, firsthand accounts, and perceptions of the city's rich naval heritage and contribution to world trade.

These written works offer a thorough understanding of Norfolk and Virginia Beach. They capture the heart and spirit of these two legendary cities, maintaining their essence for readers of every generation, whether via nuanced fiction, moving poetry, or thorough non-fiction.

Chapter 24: Iconic Norfolk and Virginia Beach Landmarks and History

Each with a rich history, Norfolk and Virginia Beach are studded with monuments that recall eras past, civic unrest, the splendor of nature, and the cultural fabric weaved over time. Here is a look at some of these cities' most recognizable landmarks and the stories they conceal:

The USS Wisconsin (BB-64) is a fearsome battleship that is currently berthed at the Nauticus museum in Norfolk. It has participated in combat during World War II, the Korean War, and the Gulf War. Ship tours provide insights into naval combat and the daily lives of enlisted sailors.

The three-mile-long Virginia Beach Boardwalk, which is decorated with sculptures and inscriptions, is more than just a strolling path. With festivals, concerts, and innumerable family trips held there throughout the years, it is a monument to the city's love of the sea.

The Norfolk Botanical Garden, a huge 175-acre garden with more than 50 themed gardens, was first a project of the Works Progress Administration in the 1930s. It provides a tranquil haven from the bustle of the city and a splash of color throughout the year.

Old Cape Henry Lighthouse: The first government funded public works project in American history, this lighthouse in

Virginia Beach has stood proudly since 1792. Visitors can ascend its spiral staircase for sweeping views of where the Atlantic Ocean and Chesapeake Bay meet.

The Norfolk-based Chrysler Museum of Art is a veritable cultural treasure trove. Over 30,000 works of art, ranging from contemporary American pop art to ancient Egyptian works, are housed there.

The Virginia Aquarium & Marine Science Center is a well-known Virginia Beach attraction that not only highlights the local marine variety but also places a strong emphasis on conservation initiatives.

General Douglas MacArthur is honored with a memorial in Norfolk that includes a museum, a research facility, and the general's ultimate burial place. It serves as a historical record of the military, especially during the World Wars.

Adam Thoroughgood House: This Virginia Beach monument offers a glimpse into English colonists' daily lives in the 1600s as one of the country's oldest still-standing colonial dwellings.

Town Point Park is Norfolk's best urban oasis and the site of numerous city-wide celebrations, festivals, and waterfront gatherings that showcase the thriving sense of community in the area.

The 34-foot-tall monument of the Roman deity Neptune in Virginia Beach is not just a photo opportunity; it also serves as a reminder of the city's close ties to the ocean.

Historic Ghent Homes: The Ghent neighborhood in Norfolk is a wonderful example of how architectural styles have evolved over time, encompassing everything from Victorian to Colonial Revival.

This park in Virginia Beach, Mount Trashmore Park, was formerly a landfill but has undergone a creative transformation. It now embodies environmental renewal thanks to the lakes, playgrounds, and skate park that have been added.

Every landmark in Norfolk and Virginia Beach, whether created by nature or constructed by man, has a history, a memory, and a story to tell. They serve as mute witnesses to history, resonating the heartbeats of all who have come before in these two illustrious cities.

Chapter 25: Architecture of Norfolk and Virginia Beach

On Virginia's coast, Norfolk and Virginia Beach are more than just close neighbors. The architectural gems that dot their landscapes reflect their shared past, which has been shaped by centuries of exploration, colonization, trade, and war. The buildings in these cities, which range from colonial homes to cutting-edge creations, tell tales of their changing social, economic, and cultural tapestries.

Beginnings of the Colonial Period: Colonial-era buildings serve as reminders of the initial settlers. A prime example is the Adam Thoroughgood House in Virginia Beach. It was constructed in the 1680s, and the English Colonial style is evident in its steep gabled roof, dormer windows, and brick chimneys.

Federal Style: Federal-style architecture began to take off in Norfolk as the country began to stand on its own after independence. With its symmetrical exterior, brick construction, and attractive yet understated ornamental accents, the Moses Myers House is proof of this.

Victorian Homes Prosper in Ghent: Victorian-era homes can be recognized by their elaborate timber trim, asymmetrical layout, and large porches in the Ghent neighborhood of Norfolk. These homes exhibit the era's love of intricate detailing and a variety of textures.

Art Deco Delights: Both cities embraced the Art Deco movement as the 20th century got underway. Buildings with streamlined facades and geometric design, like the Grayhound Bus Terminal in Norfolk, are classic examples.

The Modern and Postmodern Shift: Modernist sensibilities began to take hold by the middle of the 20th century. The highest structure in the state is the 38-story Westin Town Center in Virginia Beach. Its glass exterior, slender lines, and simple aesthetic are in keeping with the modern architectural ethos. Similar to this, Norfolk's Dominion Tower has postmodern influences with its tier-like design and reflective glass.

Beachfront Architecture: Virginia Beach's shoreline features a variety of buildings, from modest seaside cottages to imposing condos. Wide windows and balconies are frequently highlighted to enhance ocean views.

Both cities are excellent at repurposing historical sites. The Neon District in Norfolk, which was formerly a collection of outdated warehouses, is now teeming with vibrant murals, independent stores, and lofts that blend the modern and the old.

Considering their marine background, both cities have nautical undertones. A maritime-themed research center and museum called The Nauticus is located in Norfolk, and it is covered in a nautical-inspired design.

Military Imprints: Several buildings, notably in Norfolk, exhibit a utilitarian architecture as a result of their close ties to the military. The naval bases' practical, strong structures contrast sharply with the city's civilian architecture yet are an essential component of its architectural character.

Innovative Public Spaces: Urban planning has also incorporated both the modern and the ancient. While Virginia Beach's Mount Trashmore Park transforms a landfill into a recreational hub, demonstrating an innovative blend of sustainability and design, Town Point Park in Norfolk smoothly combines maritime views with urban leisure.

As a concrete record of their respective histories, both Norfolk and Virginia Beach's architecture serve as conclusions. They have created a legacy with every brick laid and window pane installed, going beyond the simple construction of buildings.

Chapter 26: Key Industries of Economic Evolution

Natural resources, a resourceful populace, and strategic geographic importance are intertwined in the economic fabric of Norfolk and Virginia Beach. They have developed into economic powerhouses as a result of significant industries that have grown, changed, and occasionally declined over time.

Maritime and shipping: The Port of Virginia has made the area a significant maritime hub with ports including Norfolk International ports (NIT) and Virginia International Gateway (VIG). Since Norfolk is the closest East Coast port to deep-water channels, it has taken advantage of this locational advantage by processing enormous amounts of containerized and breakbulk cargo annually.

Defense and Military: Naval Station Norfolk, the largest naval installation in the world, is located in Norfolk. Due to its presence, along with that of other key military stations, there are an increasing number of defense contractors, maintenance businesses, and support service providers. These organizations have supported associated businesses in technology, engineering, and logistics in addition to directly employing military personnel.

Tourism and recreation: Virginia Beach's long beachfront draws millions of tourists each year, supporting the local hospitality sector. Tourism has been a key component of the local economy because to attractions like First Landing State

Park, which honors the arrival of the first English settlers, and the famous Virginia Beach Boardwalk.

Agriculture and Aquaculture: Historically, tobacco production in the area was a good use of the fertile terrain. Soybeans, corn, and poultry were added to agriculture's diversification over time. A strong aquaculture business has also been sparked by Virginia Beach's proximity to the Atlantic, with oyster farming and fish harvesting being major contributions.

Data Centers and Technology: As the digital era began, both cities shifted their focus to become IT hubs. Data centers have been established, especially in Virginia Beach with the arrival of transatlantic cables like MAREA, underscoring the area's commitment to technological advancement.

Retail and real estate both experienced growth as populations increased and became more urbanized. With its extensive selection of stores, restaurants, and entertainment venues, Norfolk's MacArthur Center embodies the expansion of shopping in the area.

Aviation and aerospace: With adjacent institutions like the NASA Langley Research Center and a wide range of support firms, the aerospace sector has contributed to the region's economic diversification.

Education and healthcare are becoming major jobs thanks to establishments like Norfolk's Old Dominion University and Eastern Virginia Medical School. Their presence has also contributed to an increase in start-ups and enterprises focused on research.

Energy and sustainability: Virginia Beach has financed sustainability initiatives in response to the global transition to renewable energy. Offshore wind farms are now under development and have great promise as a key energy and employment source in the years to come.

In conclusion, Norfolk and Virginia Beach's economic development is evidence of their capacity for innovation and adaptation. Their expansion from their maritime beginnings into a variety of contemporary sectors has ensured their sustained importance in the larger national scene.

Chapter 27: Norfolk and Virginia Beach in the National and Global Economy

Long-standing economic powerhouses in Virginia, Norfolk and Virginia Beach have also left their mark on the country and the world. These cities have been able to make major contributions and play key roles in more general economic narratives thanks to their positioning, both strategically and geographically.

Port of Virginia, sometimes known as the "Gateway to the World," is located in Norfolk and is one of the biggest and busiest ports on the American East Coast. Some of the largest cargo ships in the world can fit in its deep waters. The port, which serves as a crucial entry point to global markets, manages enormous volumes of containerized, breakbulk, bulk, and roll-on/roll-off cargo, connecting American companies with markets in Europe, Asia, and other regions of the world. On a national level, it is essential in sustaining the U.S. trade deficit by managing the imports and exports that drive the economy.

Strength in Defense - Naval Station Norfolk Norfolk makes a significant contribution to the U.S. defense infrastructure as the location of the largest naval facility in the world. In addition to influencing domestic defense policies, the military personnel stationed here has a worldwide geopolitical impact through the defense contracts carried out, the navy vessels and aircraft maintained and deployed from this facility.

Transatlantic Digital Corridor: Virginia Beach has evolved into a digital gateway between North America, Europe, and beyond with the installation of the MAREA and BRUSA transatlantic cables there. These cables, which provide high-speed internet connections, put Virginia Beach—and subsequently the United States—at the center of international digital communication and data transfer, a crucial component of the current information-driven global economy.

Greater Impact of Tourism: Virginia Beach's tourism business draws tourists from all over the world in addition to locals. The financial impact of this industry is more extensive. As it promotes American culture and hospitality to foreign tourists, it helps the nation's tax receipts, supports the airline and travel businesses, and strengthens the soft power of the United States.

Exports of agricultural products: Products from the area, such seafood caught in the Atlantic or agriculture from the region's lush soils, are consumed on a national and international scale. The U.S.'s position in the world fish trade has been strengthened by the considerable export of seafood, particularly from Virginia Beach.

Education and Research Outreach: Norfolk-area universities and medical schools including Eastern Virginia Medical School and Old Dominion University participate in partnerships and exchange programs with universities throughout the world. By encouraging international cooperation in research, science, and cultural exchange, they support the United States' soft power.

Global Green Initiatives: By investing in renewable energy, especially the construction of offshore wind farms, Virginia Beach is putting itself and the country at the forefront of international sustainability initiatives.

In conclusion, despite appearing to be only two small points on the enormous US map, Norfolk and Virginia Beach make significant contributions to both the domestic and international economies. Their strategic advancements over the years have made sure that their power reverberates well beyond the boundaries of their city, influencing narratives in the fields of economics, defense, and culture on bigger stages.

Chapter 28: Notable Companies in Norfolk and Virginia Beach

Given their important positions and lengthy histories, Norfolk and Virginia Beach have never just been seaside cities. These regions have supported and housed several businesses over the years that have not only increased the region's economic development but also left their mark on the national and occasionally international scene. Here are a few of the well-known organizations that have resided in these cities:

Company name: Norfolk Southern One of the main providers of transportation in the country, this Fortune 500 firm has its corporate headquarters in Norfolk. With a long history dating back to the 1800s, Norfolk Southern has a significant presence in the Eastern United States, where it runs one of the largest freight railroads and provides comprehensive logistics services.

Huntington Ingalls Industries (Newport News Shipbuilding): Despite having its headquarters in Newport News, it is a major employer in the area due to its proximity to Norfolk and shared workforce. It is both the largest shipbuilding enterprise in the US and the largest industrial employment in Virginia, producing mainly ships for the US Navy and Coast Guard.

Smithfield Foods: Based in Virginia Beach, Smithfield is the biggest producer and processor of hogs and pork in the world. It is a household name in meat production and ships its goods both domestically and abroad.

Chainsaws, blowers, trimmers, and other handheld outdoor power tools are among the products made by Virginia Beach-based STIHL Inc. The business has significantly boosted the regional economy and is well known for its cutting-edge goods.

Government Employees Insurance Company, or GEICO, has a sizable regional office in Virginia Beach with thousands of employees there. The massive provider of auto insurance is well-known around the country for its ads and is well-established in the area.

AMSEC LLC: AMSEC is a naval architecture and marine engineering company that was first founded in Virginia Beach. Its offerings have grown over time to include mission assurance, technical support for naval ships, and other defense-related services.

Optima Health: With roots in Norfolk and Virginia Beach, this company offers health plan coverage to a wide range of members, including families, businesses, and individuals.

Dominion Enterprises: With its headquarters in Norfolk, Dominion Enterprises provides publishing alternatives and cloud-based B2B technology solutions. Their influence extends to the automobile, marine, and real estate industries.

System engineering, in-service engineering, and training are just a few of the services provided by Virginia Beach-based Valkyrie Enterprises, LLC, to the U.S. Defense industry.

Virginia Natural Gas (VNG), a subsidiary of Southern Company Gas with headquarters in Virginia Beach, serves the southeast portion of Virginia, including Norfolk and the surrounding area, with natural gas service.

Despite the fact that these are only a few instances, it is obvious that Norfolk and Virginia Beach have developed a broad economic ecosystem. These businesses demonstrate the region's economic adaptability and vigor by representing a variety of sectors, including consumer products, healthcare, and the transportation and defense industries.

Chapter 29: Visual Art and Movements in Norfolk and Virginia Beach

In Norfolk and Virginia Beach, which have long been centers of culture, art is not only valued but also profoundly ingrained in the development and history of the locals. These cities have vibrant, diverse, and over time, drastically changing visual arts scenes.

The Chrysler Museum of Art is a significant American art museum with more than 30,000 pieces. It is situated in Norfolk. They cover a long period of time and include ancient art, European and American paintings, sculptures, decorative arts, and glass. Particularly the museum's glass collection is well known all over the world.

Neon District: Located in Norfolk's central business district, the Neon (New Energy of Norfolk) District is a culturally rich area well-known for its outdoor murals, public artwork, and cultural activities. This area exemplifies the city's dedication to public art and its revitalization through the arts.

The Virginia Museum of Contemporary Art (MOCA) is a showcase for the contemporary art movements that have flourished in the region. It is located in Virginia Beach. With a variety of shows that change throughout the year, it highlights important national and regional artists.

The D'Art Center, which is situated in Norfolk's NEON District, has played a significant role in the city's history since the 1980s. In addition to offering working artists studio space, the center frequently hosts interactive sessions and seminars to involve the local population.

The ViBe Creative District in Virginia Beach supports regional artists, craftspeople, and companies that cater to the creative industry. This neighborhood is filled with murals, sculptures, and community art initiatives that encourage creativity.

Projects involving Public Art: Virginia Beach has embraced the usage of Public Art in Public Places. Art has been used to enhance public places, from the "Wave" sculpture in the Laskin Road Roundabout to different statues along the boardwalk and pathways.

The Art Institute of Virginia Beach has contributed to shaping and supporting the local art scene by nurturing creativity and providing academic training while also bringing new ideas and abilities to the fore.

Local art galleries: There are many art galleries in Norfolk and Virginia Beach that include both homegrown artists and artists from other cities. The Mayer Fine Art Gallery and the Gallery 21 in Norfolk are notable locations that frequently feature the newest contemporary art movements.

Annual art events are held in both cities, including the Boardwalk Art Show in Virginia Beach, one of the best outdoor fine art exhibitions on the Eastern Shore and one of the oldest.

Influence of the Naval History: It is hardly surprising that marine themes are common in local art given Norfolk's considerable naval history. There is no denying the connection between the city's naval history and its art, whether it be in murals, sculptures, or even items from nearby galleries.

In Norfolk and Virginia Beach, a vibrant arts community has been cultivated by this complex tapestry of organizations, neighborhoods, and activities. The region's art, which ranges from the classical to the contemporary, not only represents its rich history and varied culture but also prepares the way for upcoming artistic undertakings.

Chapter 30: Music and Musical Movements in Norfolk and Virginia Beach

Both Norfolk and Virginia Beach have fostered vibrant musical traditions that range from classical to hip-hop, ensuring that both communities are important players in the larger American musical scene. The region's dynamic communities and coastline attractiveness have provided a setting for both musical creativity and preservation.

The Norfolk Sound is a kind of music that first appeared in the 1960s and is distinguished by its fusion of soul, R&B, and beach music. This sound was largely shaped by producers like Frank Guida, with singles like Gary U.S. Bonds' "Quarter to Three" perfectly encapsulating the mood of the time.

Hip-Hop and R&B: Some of the genres' most important figures call Virginia Beach and Norfolk home. These musicians, including Timbaland, Missy Elliott, and Pharrell Williams, have produced tunes that have reached the top of the charts and changed the course of modern music. These regional artists are occasionally featured at the Neptune Festival in Virginia Beach as a tribute to their roots.

Orchestral and Classical Movements: The Norfolk-based Virginia Symphony Orchestra has been a mainstay of classical music in the area for more than a century. It was established in 1921 and has consistently given local audiences performances of both classical masterpieces and modern compositions.

The gospel tradition: Given that the South is home to gospel music, it is not surprising that the genre has strong roots there. Spirited gospel performances that combine music and spirituality have frequently been held at churches in Norfolk and Virginia Beach.

Influence of jazz and the blues: The Attucks Theatre in Norfolk, also referred to as the "Apollo of the South," was a crucial stop on the Chitlin' Circuit. The city's prominence in jazz and blues history was cemented by the presence on its stage of legends like Duke Ellington, Cab Calloway, and Mamie Smith.

Music festivals: One of the biggest outdoor music gatherings on the East Coast is the American Music Festival in Virginia Beach, which features performances in a variety of musical genres, from rock to jazz, country to R&B, and everything in between. Similar to this, Norfolk's Bayou Boogaloo Music & Cajun Food Festival honors New Orleans' voluminous musical and gastronomic heritage.

Music Venues: In addition to festivals, places like the NorVa in Norfolk, which was formerly a vaudeville theater and is now one of the best concert venues in the nation, have played host to a number of spectacular performances, ranging from up-and-coming regional bands to world-renowned artists.

Education in music: Organizations like Norfolk's Old Dominion University have promoted music education. Its music department, which offers a wide variety of curricula, has played a crucial role in developing the following generation of musicians and teachers.

Local Radio and Music Shows: Regional music has long been strongly supported by local radio. With programming devoted to different genres, radio stations like WHRO-FM make sure that the local sound is heard everywhere in the neighborhood.

Folk and Country Traditions: It should come as no surprise that both cities have vibrant folk and country music cultures given their Southern history. These genres are frequently included at neighborhood taverns, events, and fairs, reflecting the region's varied musical tastes.

Music continues to play a significant role in the local culture in Norfolk and Virginia Beach thanks to its long history and cutting-edge advancements. The contributions of the cities are heard on both the national and international stages, demonstrating that their musical history is still as alive as ever.

Chapter 31: Other Cultural Festivals in Norfolk and Virginia Beach

Due to their advantageous coastal positions and lengthy histories, Norfolk and Virginia Beach are cultural melting pots. The numerous events held throughout the year vividly display this diversity. These festivals give locals and visitors alike the chance to fully immerse themselves in the dynamic fabric of the area, from culinary delicacies to musical feasts, from traditional commemorations to modern revelries.

Every year, Norfolk's Town Point Park is transformed into a vivacious bayou to celebrate the tastes, sounds, and dynamic energy of New Orleans during the Bayou Boogaloo Music & Cajun Food Festival. Three days of Cajun specialties, craft brews, and jazz to zydeco music are all part of the festival.

The Festival of Neptune: This festival honors Virginia Beach's marine heritage and is held there every year. It's a must-attend festival that draws hundreds of thousands of people and features over 35 events, including an international sand sculpting competition, an arts and crafts market, and the Neptune Grand Parade.

The Virginia Arts Festival is a notable occasion that draws artists from all over the world to Norfolk. Every spring, the Virginia Arts Festival presents a wide range of artistic undertakings, from classical music to theatrical productions.

Norfolk Harborfest: This three-day free event honors the city's long nautical history and features tall ship exhibitions, the biggest fireworks display on the East Coast, and a procession of sails.

Pungo Strawberry Festival: This celebration of local agriculture is held in Virginia Beach over Memorial Day weekend. A family-friendly festival, it features strawberry picking, pie eating competitions, carnival attractions, and a military demonstration, drawing visitors from all across the state.

The festival honoring Filipino and American friendship: This festival honors the sizeable Filipino community in Virginia Beach by showcasing traditional dances, dishes, and performances.

Jewish Film Festival: This festival, which is run in association with the Simon Family JCC in Virginia Beach, features independent and foreign films that examine Jewish history, culture, and life.

Festival of the Arts at Stockley Gardens: This festival, which is held twice a year in Norfolk's historic Ghent area, has live music, cuisine, and kid-friendly activities in addition to the artwork of over 130 artists.

PrideFest: PrideFest, which honors the LGBTQ+ population in Norfolk, blends entertainment, shopping, and good times with advocacy, making it one of the most inclusive (and biggest) festivals in the area.

The Latino Music Festival in Virginia Beach features a fusion of traditional and modern Latino music, dancing performances, and gastronomic delights for festival goers.

The East Coast She-Crab Soup Classic is a food festival in Virginia Beach where local eateries compete for the title of "Best She-Crab Soup" by serving their own unique takes on the region's hallmark dish.

Along with other events, these festivals contribute to Norfolk and Virginia Beach's cultural vibrancy. Each event strengthens the sense of belonging, inclusivity, and celebration that the area is renowned for while also providing a glimpse into the rich tapestry of traditions and arts.

Chapter 32: Key Educational Institutions

Within the larger Hampton Roads metropolitan area, Norfolk and Virginia Beach have developed into important hubs for education on the East Coast. Here is a look at some of the most important educational institutions that have influenced people's thinking, promoted research, and made a substantial contribution to the social and economic fabric of the area.

Old Dominion University (ODU): Founded in 1930 and based in Norfolk, ODU has made a name for itself as a significant center for research. The institution, which has approximately 24,000 students as residents, provides a wide range of studies in the sciences, arts, business, and engineering. International attention has been drawn to its contribution to research, notably in fields like climate change and sea level rise.

Norfolk State institution is a public institution that was established in 1935 and provides a thorough education. It has a long history of promoting African-American education and continues to be dedicated to making higher education accessible and affordable.

On the border of Virginia Beach and Norfolk, Virginia Wesleyan University offers a small-class size learning environment with a focus on undergraduate research and civic involvement.

One of the biggest community schools in Virginia is Tidewater Community College (TCC), which has campuses all across the area, including one in Virginia Beach and another in Norfolk. It provides a wide range of programs to meet the different needs of the Hampton Roads community, ranging from conventional undergraduate courses to specialized training programs.

Eastern Virginia Medical School (EVMS), a Norfolk-based institution, has distinguished itself in the field of medical education. Along with educating medical professionals, it also actively participates in community health programs and ground-breaking scientific research.

Dr. Pat Robertson established Virginia Beach-based Regent University as a private Christian institution in 1977. It offers a wide range of undergraduate, graduate, and doctorate programs with a focus on leadership and a Christian view of education.

One of the oldest educational institutions in the nation, Norfolk Academy is an independent co-educational day school that was established in 1728. The institution, which serves children in kindergarten through twelfth grade, has a strong reputation for academic excellence and all-around student growth.

One of Virginia's largest public school systems, Virginia Beach City Public Schools serves the different educational needs of the city's residents. The district is renowned for its technical advancements, innovative programs, and emphasis on educating kids for a globalized society.

Norfolk Collegiate School: This private day school in Norfolk was founded in 1948 and offers a full curriculum from kindergarten through twelfth grade. It guarantees a well-rounded educational experience by placing a heavy emphasis on technology, the arts, and sports.

When it comes to the academic diversity of Norfolk and Virginia Beach, these academic institutions are merely the tip of the iceberg. By guaranteeing that local students have access to top-notch education, they encourage a culture of intellectual curiosity and lifelong learning.

Chapter 33: Norfolk and Virginia Beach's Role in Academia and Research

Norfolk and Virginia Beach have developed past their historic and maritime beginnings to become centers of academic excellence and research over time. Their research facilities, institutions, and partnerships with the public and commercial sectors guarantee that they play a significant role on the national and international academic scene.

Climate and marine research: Given their proximity to the ocean, Norfolk and Virginia Beach have both prioritized marine research. With research facilities devoted to coping with sea level rise and climate change, Old Dominion University (ODU) is at the vanguard. The Climate Change and Sea Level Rise Initiative (CCSLRI) at Ohio Dominican University is dedicated to multidisciplinary research and cooperates with governmental organizations.

Medical Innovations: The Eastern Virginia Medical School (EVMS) has continuously pushed the limits of medicine. It has been a pioneer in a number of research fields, particularly reproductive medicine. The nation's first in-vitro fertilization was accomplished at the Jones Institute for Reproductive Medicine at EVMS, and the first IVF baby was born there in 1981 as a result.

Engineering and technology: At ODU, the Frank Batten College of Engineering and Technology is a major force behind research and technological advancements in fields including robotics, bioelectricity, and cybersecurity. Their innovative work frequently involves collaboration with defense agencies, which reflects the region's military importance.

Economic and social research: Due to the region's thriving economy, many projects are being undertaken that concentrate on socioeconomic trends. ODU's Dragas Center for Economic Analysis and Policy frequently offers analysis on local employment, housing, and economic developments.

Collaborations with NASA have been facilitated by the area's proximity to NASA's Langley Research Center, particularly with ODU. Research in fields like atmospheric science and aerospace has been the focus of joint partnerships.

study on culture and history: Because the area has a long history, numerous institutions—including local colleges and museums—engage in active historical study. Focus has been placed on the recording and preservation of colonial history, maritime history, and the Civil Rights struggle.

Environmental protection: In addition to being a well-known tourist destination, the Virginia Aquarium & Marine Science Center in Virginia Beach serves as a hub for marine research. It delivers educational programs on marine biodiversity and actively encourages conservation initiatives.

Research in defense and security: Given Norfolk's substantial military presence, this field naturally attracts attention. Collaborations between military installations and academic institutions lead to improvements in defense tactics, battle simulations, and naval engineering.

Public health Research: The varied populations of Norfolk and Virginia Beach make it an appropriate location for public health research. Studies on infectious illnesses, health inequities, and community health are routinely conducted at EVMS and other institutions.

In conclusion, Norfolk and Virginia Beach are pillars of academic and research excellence in the country. They provide more than just attractive scenery and naval sites. Universities, governmental organizations, and the corporate sector work together in a synergistic way to increase their contribution to world knowledge.

Chapter 34: Natural Disasters in Norfolk and Virginia Beach and their Impact

Due to their coastal settings, Norfolk and Virginia Beach have had their fair share of natural disasters. These incidents have had a substantial impact on the infrastructure, regulations, and resilience plans for the area over time.

Hurricanes and Tropical Storms: Because Norfolk and Virginia Beach are coastal communities, they have both experienced the brunt of countless hurricanes and tropical storms.

One of the worst was Hurricane Isabel (2003), which caused extensive floods, power disruptions, and substantial property damage. Particularly severe flooding resulted from the storm surge, with water levels in some places rising by several feet.

Despite not being as strong as Hurricane Isabel, Hurricane Matthew (2016) nonetheless caused significant flooding in both cities, exposing flaws in drainage and flood control systems.

Tidal flooding and Sea-Level Rise: Sea-level rise is a distinct and complicated problem that is mostly caused by climate change. Particularly on the East Coast, Norfolk is seeing some of the highest rates of sea-level rise. Flooding referred to as "sunny day" or "nuisance" is becoming common, especially in low-lying areas.

Nor'easters: Although less well-known than hurricanes, nor'easters can nevertheless cause significant wind, flooding, and coastal erosion damage. The storm in 2009 stands significance because it significantly increased flooding in Norfolk and Virginia Beach and gave stormwater management systems newfound attention.

Snowfall & Winter Storms: Although the area is better recognized for its mild temperature, severe winter weather can nevertheless strike there. In some areas, the 1980 blizzard dumped over a foot of snow, rendering several cities inoperable for days.

Although uncommon, the area does occasionally experience earthquakes. Despite being centered northwest of Richmond, the 2011 Virginia earthquake was powerfully felt in Norfolk and Virginia Beach, alarming many but only causing little damage.

These natural calamities have an effect that goes beyond just bodily harm. They've had an impact on urban planning, resulting in:

Infrastructure Improvements: To accommodate storm surges and heavy rains, the cities have upgraded flood walls, storm drains, and pumping stations.

Establishing and disseminating evacuation routes and protocols has received a lot of attention given to the area's vulnerability to hurricanes.

Initiatives for building resilience against sea-level rise and greater flooding have been launched in both cities. Plans for living shorelines, sea walls, and updated building rules for new structures are all included in this.

Public education initiatives: Cities regularly run public awareness programs on how citizens may get ready for various natural catastrophes because they understand how important community preparedness is.

In conclusion, despite the difficulties caused by multiple natural catastrophes, Norfolk and Virginia Beach have benefited from these occurrences in terms of creativity, community togetherness, and resilience tactics. The cities are always changing and adapting to keep their inhabitants safe and happy.

Chapter 35: History of Sports and Athletes from Norfolk and Virginia Beach

With a long history of producing outstanding athletes and holding prestigious sporting events, Norfolk and Virginia Beach have carved out a unique niche for themselves in the sporting world. These cities' athletic path has been marked by successes on the national stage, the construction of sports facilities, and the development of sports communities.

Early Sports Beginnings: Baseball grew in popularity in the area during the late 19th and early 20th century. A minor league baseball team called the Norfolk Tars competed in the Piedmont League before moving on to the Virginia League. Their games were well-attended occasions that attracted a lot of local support.

Basketball: Basketball also left its influence, particularly after the Norfolk Scope Arena hosted the Virginia Squires of the American Basketball Association. Early in their careers, greats like George Gervin and Julius "Dr. J" Erving were a part of the club.

Football: Despite the absence of an NFL team in Norfolk or Virginia Beach, the region has produced world-class football players. One of the most noteworthy is Bruce Smith, a Norfolk native who played 19 NFL seasons and was inducted into the Hall of Fame as one of the league's finest defensive ends.

Soccer: The Virginia Beach Mariners gave the sport a local professional presence in the 1990s and 2000s by competing in the United Soccer Leagues First Division, but the team eventually disbanded in 2007.

Tennis: The Virginia Beach Tennis and Country Club has served as a training ground for aspiring tennis stars as well as the site of major national competitions.

Water Sports: Given the seaside locations of the cities, activities like swimming, sailing, and surfing have always been popular choices. One of the oldest surfing competitions in North America is held each year at Virginia Beach, namely, where the East Coast Surfing Championships are held.

Athletes of Note: In addition to Bruce Smith, the following athletes have become well-known in the area:

Alonzo Mourning: The NBA Hall of Famer was born in Chesapeake and played high school basketball in Virginia. He spent a large portion of his career with the Miami Heat.

Gabby Douglas: This Olympic gymnastics gold medallist hails from Virginia Beach, as was previously said.

Pernell "Sweet Pea" Whitaker, a boxer who won an Olympic gold medal and later won four world championship titles, was born in Norfolk.

Ryan Zimmerman is a well-known MLB player who plays for the Washington Nationals. He was born in Washington, North Carolina, but moved to Virginia Beach as a young man.

Sports Facilities: Stadiums, arenas, and sports complexes were all developed as a result of the rise and interest in sports. A good example is the Norfolk Scope Arena, which hosts many events as well as basketball and ice hockey.

Running & marathons: The cities have long been a favorite for marathons and half-marathons thanks to their picturesque coastal courses. The Virginia Beach Shamrock Marathon is a well-known occasion that attracts people from all across the nation.

The history of Norfolk and Virginia Beach are profoundly entwined with athletics, to sum up. The cities continue to celebrate and cultivate athletic talent, from creating world-class athletes to hosting nationally renowned events, and have become an integral part of Virginia's larger sporting narrative.

Chapter 36: Noteworthy Recreational Spaces

There are numerous leisure spaces available in Norfolk and Virginia Beach thanks to their rich coastal geography and urban development. Locals and visitors alike find comfort and activity in these settings, from verdant parks to peaceful beaches.

Three miles of Virginia Beach's oceanfront make up what may be the city's most recognizable recreation area. With its boardwalk, which is adorned with monuments, eateries, and live music, it is a lively scene all year long. Numerous celebrations and events, including the Neptune Festival, are also held in the area.

First Landing State Park is a 2,888-acre state park in Virginia Beach that is situated where the first English settlers arrived in the area in 1607. It provides camping, hiking, and beach amenities. It is a refuge for those who love the outdoors because of its variety of landscapes, from dunes to marshes.

The 175-acre Norfolk Botanical Garden is a vibrant and tranquil sanctuary in the middle of the city. It provides tourists with a revitalizing experience with themed gardens like the Japanese Garden and the Rose Garden. The garden is particularly well-known for its boat trips and butterfly house.

Mount Trashmore Park was built in Virginia Beach on the site of a former landfill, which is a creative use of space. It is now a busy area with lakes, skate parks, and hiking trails. Families particularly enjoy this playground, called Kids Cove.

The 10.5-mile Elizabeth River Trail, which connects communities and showcases Norfolk's coastline, is a popular urban bike and walking route. It provides beautiful Elizabeth River views, historic locations, and metropolitan scenes.

Town Point Park, located in the heart of Norfolk, serves as a gathering place for public performances, festivals, and activities. It's the ideal location for picnics, strolls, and taking in the city skyline because it overlooks the waterfront.

False Cape State Park, located in southern Virginia Beach, offers a more wild and isolated experience and is only reachable by boat, bicycle, or foot. At the point where the Back Bay meets the Atlantic Ocean, it provides a spotless beach, hiking paths, and a distinctive setting.

Locals also refer to Chesapeake Bay Beach as "Chick's Beach" as it is a more serene option to the oceanfront. It's perfect for children and people seeking to escape the hustle and bustle because of the calmer waters and less tourists.

Lakewood Park in Norfolk has beautiful water views, lots of open area for outdoor leisure, and a playground for kids.

The Adventure Park at Virginia Aquarium is a park in Virginia Beach that combines adventure and environment by providing zip lines and treetop pathways. Both beginners and those looking for adventure can use it because it is made for different ability levels.

Essentially, Norfolk and Virginia Beach offer a diverse range of recreational areas. These cities' parks and recreational places meet all demands, whether one is interested in history, nature, or simply wants to unwind. This reflects the cities' dedication to environmental sustainability, heritage, and communal well-being.

Chapter 37: Noteworthy Nature in Norfolk and Virginia Beach

The Coastal Virginia region, which includes Norfolk and Virginia Beach, is home to a wide variety of natural treasures. These cities are havens for nature enthusiasts due to the convergence of rivers, the Chesapeake Bay, the Atlantic Ocean, and the region's unique ecosystems.

Back Bay National Wildlife Refuge in Virginia Beach features a rare combination of beach, dunes, woods, and freshwater marshes over a land area of approximately 9,000 acres. Visitors may see endangered animals like the loggerhead sea turtle or the tundra swan at this sanctuary for migratory birds.

The Elizabeth River is more than just a stream as it meanders through Norfolk. The Learning Barge, restored wetlands, and the Paradise Creek Nature Park have all been added as part of the Elizabeth River Project's restoration efforts, transforming some of the river into a living classroom.

First Landing State Park: Here, kayakers can observe the park's varied wildlife, which includes over 60 species of neotropical migratory birds, against a hauntingly beautiful backdrop of bald cypress swamps.

House of Pleasure Point:

This 118-acre salt marsh in Virginia Beach is an important habitat for coastal bird species and is considered a coastal environmental treasure. The Brock Environmental Center, a pioneer in sustainable architecture and environmental education, is also located there.

The Norfolk Botanical Garden is a showcase for horticulture and design, but it also acts as a natural environment. Children can explore coastal habitats, desert landscapes, and more inside the World of Wonders - A Children's Adventure Garden.

The Chesapeake Bay: The Bay provides homes for a variety of aquatic life thanks to its tidal inlets and salt marshes. Particularly noteworthy is Virginia Beach's Lynnhaven Inlet, which was formerly well-known for its Lynnhaven oysters.

The 42-acre Lake Lawson/Lake Smith Natural Area in Virginia Beach is made up of freshwater tidal marshes and woodlands. Freshwater fishing enthusiasts flock to these two lakes, and birdwatchers can view a wide variety of wading birds and ducks there.

Lafayette River: The once-heavily polluted Lafayette River in Norfolk has experienced a comeback. Oyster restoration initiatives have improved the water's quality, enabling river otters, ospreys, and occasionally dolphins to live there.

False A rare unspoiled wilderness, Cape State Park is home to a wide variety of creatures, from wild horses to fiddler crabs. It is a snapshot of the original coastal Virginia scenery because of how isolated it is, which has retained its pure character.

Hoffler Creek Wildlife Preserve is a 142-acre preserve in Portsmouth, close to Norfolk, that contains a variety of ecosystems, from old-growth forests to tidal estuaries. It serves as a haven for many bird species, deer, and foxes.

In conclusion, Norfolk and Virginia Beach have a wide variety of natural ecosystems and landscapes. Every natural area has a tale to tell about preservation, history, and striking a balance between advancing cities and ecological preservation. These oases provide solace to both tourists and locals, serving as a reminder to preserve the region's natural legacy for future generations.

Chapter 38: Environmental Issues in Norfolk and Virginia Beach

Even Norfolk and Virginia Beach, two coastal communities with a long history of development, have experienced the effects of environmental problems. These cities deal with specific environmental problems that affect both their natural ecosystems and their urban environments as the effects of human activity and shifting global conditions grow increasingly obvious.

Sea-Level Rise: Norfolk and Virginia Beach are immediately affected by the dangers of increasing sea levels because they are both located in the Atlantic coastline zone. The region faces one of the highest rates of relative sea-level rise on the U.S. East Coast as a result of a combination of global sea-level rise, sinking land, and the Gulf Stream's changing patterns. As a result, there have been several instances of tidal flooding, endangering buildings, infrastructure, and natural habitats.

Concerns about water quality: The Elizabeth River, which flows through Norfolk, has a history of pollution problems. Although there have been major restoration attempts, industrial contaminants from the past, such as polychlorinated biphenyls (PCBs), continue to be of concern. Similar effects on oyster populations and overall water quality have been caused by runoff from urban areas into waterways like the Lynnhaven River in Virginia Beach.

Loss of Wetlands: Wetlands are essential for ecosystems and for flood control. However, they have been in danger because of urbanization, a rise in sea levels, and alterations in the quality of the water. There are currently efforts being done to restore these priceless ecosystems, yet difficulties still exist.

Air quality Problems: Norfolk and Virginia Beach occasionally have elevated ozone levels as a result of growing urbanization and motor traffic, particularly during the busiest travel seasons. Despite being usually regarded as having high air quality, ozone standard deviations can occasionally endanger the health of vulnerable populations.

Threat to Biodiversity: A wide range of species are supported by the diverse habitats, which range from freshwater marshes to coastal dunes. The area flora and animals are threatened by pollution, climate change, and deterioration of habitat, which results in a loss of biodiversity.

garbage management: As populations and tourist numbers rise, more garbage is produced. To stop land and water contamination, effective waste management, recycling, and a decrease in single-use plastics are continuous problems.

Urban Heat Islands: Because of their concrete buildings and asphalt roads, cities have a tendency to absorb heat and then radiate it back into the surrounding area, raising localized temperatures. This phenomena and its effects on energy use and public health must be understood by Norfolk and Virginia Beach as they grow and urbanize.

Challenges in Resilience and Adaptation: Both cities are in a race against time to adapt given the challenges, particularly from sea-level rise and rising storm intensity. It is vital to make investments in robust infrastructure, eco-friendly solutions, and neighborhood education.

Both Norfolk and Virginia Beach have experienced a rise in community involvement, policy reform, and creative solutions as a result of these environmental issues. To assure a sustainable future for these coastal treasures, grassroots organizations, local government, and academic institutions are working together. The trip is still ongoing, but it is clear that there is a desire to safeguard and preserve.

Chapter 39: Technological Advancements from Norfolk and Virginia Beach

In addition to its historical significance and stunning natural surroundings, Norfolk and Virginia Beach have served as hubs for technological development and innovation. Despite not often being linked with the tech booms that are common in locations like Silicon Valley, the area has made significant contributions in a number of different disciplines because to the efforts of local organizations, companies, and people.

Naval Innovation: It's not surprise that many of the technology developments have ties to marine operations given Norfolk's importance as a naval hub. Modernizing military vessels, creating cutting-edge shipbuilding methods, and applying cutting-edge naval engineering have all been made possible thanks in large part to the Norfolk military Shipyard.

Space and Satellite Technology: Though not exclusively developed in Virginia Beach or Norfolk, the larger Virginia region has seen numerous professionals and businesses engaged in aerospace technology contribute significantly to advancements in satellite tech and space exploration. This is due to its proximity to NASA Langley Research Center and Wallops Flight Facility.

Health and Medical Technologies: With the availability of renowned medical facilities like Sentara Norfolk General Hospital, there has been a push to use cutting-edge medical technology to improve patient care, from telemedicine to the use of cutting-edge medical imaging devices and robotic surgery.

Contributions from digital and IT: The presence of colleges and universities in and near Norfolk and Virginia Beach, such Old Dominion University, has encouraged expansion in the IT industry. Startups and IT firms that focus on software development, cybersecurity, and data analytics have grown rapidly in the area.

Green technologies: Given the region's environmental difficulties, particularly those related to sea level rise, there has been a strong emphasis on environmentally friendly technology. The area is committed to using technology to tackle environmental problems, from creating cutting-edge stormwater management systems to green building practices.

Tourism and AR/VR: Due to Virginia Beach's robust tourism business, augmented reality (AR) and virtual reality (VR) have been integrated to improve the visitor experience. The way tourists experience the area is changing as a result of technology, from virtual museum tours to AR beach trails.

Agricultural Technology: There is a significant agricultural presence in the regions surrounding Norfolk and Virginia Beach. Precision farming, the usage of drones, and sustainable aquaculture are examples of agritech breakthroughs that have their roots in local experts' and institutions' innovations and practices.

Although Norfolk and Virginia Beach may not frequently be mentioned in the news as IT centers, their influence on technology is indisputable. Their maritime tradition, academic institutions, and the difficulties posed by their location have combined to create a unique atmosphere that has inspired innovation and advancement.

Chapter 40: The Future Outlook for Norfolk and Virginia Beach

Given their rich history, strategic location, and natural resources, Norfolk and Virginia Beach are projected to have a diverse future that takes into account both the past and the present as well as what lies in the future.

Environmental Resilience: Norfolk and Virginia Beach will be at the forefront of the fight against coastal flooding and its effects as sea levels rise globally. To lessen the effects, it is anticipated that investments in green infrastructure, cutting-edge stormwater management systems, and creative urban planning would rise. Projects like "Living with Water" emphasize the direction toward a resilient future.

Technology Hub: By leveraging their academic and military institutions, Norfolk and Virginia Beach are ready to increase their technological footprint. A burgeoning startup culture is to be anticipated, strengthened by government assistance and partnerships with organizations like Norfolk State University and Old Dominion University.

Tourism Evolution: Virginia Beach, already well-known for its outdoor attractions and beaches, is anticipated to further advance the visitor experience. Beyond the physical attractions, immersive digital experiences like augmented and virtual reality tours will transform travel.

Transition to Green Energy: Both cities are likely to adopt green energy strategies more comprehensively. Investments in renewable energy sources, such as solar panels and wind turbines, are expected to soar, making the cities leaders in the use of sustainable energy.

Port and Naval Expansion: Taking advantage of developments in international trade, the Port of Virginia in Norfolk, one of the most prominent on the East Coast, may undergo modifications and expansions. Given the worldwide geopolitical changes, the naval bases might also undergo expansions or strategic reevaluations.

Cultural Renewal: Both cities, which have a rich tapestry of history and culture, are anticipated to experience a cultural renaissance. The local scene will probably be enhanced by new museums, art galleries, and cultural festivals that celebrate diversity.

While the port, naval base, and tourism industries predominate, there is a clear trend toward economic diversification. A shift toward a more balanced economy may be seen in the expansion of the tech industry, the healthcare industry, and educational institutions.

Urban Development and Housing: As a result of population expansion and shifting demographics, urban development initiatives that prioritize green areas, affordable housing, and public transportation are likely to gain traction.

Enhancing connection is a priority for enhanced transportation networks. To better handle the growing traffic and connect neighborhoods, anticipate improved road networks, prospective light rail expansions, and perhaps new bridges.

In conclusion, Norfolk and Virginia Beach have a promising future ahead of them, filled with chances and obstacles that will highlight their importance to the country and put their resiliency to the test. The cities are prepared for expansion, adaptability, and innovation as they carry on the resilience and evolution of the past.

Chapter 41: Must-See Locations in Norfolk and Virginia Beach

Norfolk:

The Battleship and Nauticus Wisconsin: This science center and museum with a maritime theme is a delight for all ages. The USS Wisconsin, a huge battleship that served in WWII, is displayed in the center.

The nearly 150-acre Norfolk Botanical Garden is a year-round destination with themed gardens, including a Japanese garden and a rose garden.

The Chrysler Museum of Art is the repository of a vast collection that includes more than 30,000 items from more than 5,000 years of human history. A renowned glass collection and on-site glass studio are additional features of the museum.

The Virginia Zoo is a place where you may observe animals including lions, kangaroos, and elephants. It is situated in Lafayette Park.

Historic Ghent District: Known for its residences, shops, and restaurants from the early 20th century. The Harrison Opera House is another building in the neighborhood.

The Neon District is Norfolk's cultural hub, home to several murals, sculptures, and a burgeoning nightlife.

Virginia Beach:

The three-mile-long Virginia Beach Boardwalk is a well-known attraction that features statues, stages for live entertainment, and access to the Atlantic Ocean's sandy shoreline.

Aquarium and Marine Science Center of Virginia This institution exhibits aquatic life, such as sea turtles, sharks, and rays, and is a great family destination.

The exact location of the English colonists' first landing in 1607 is preserved at First Landing State Park. It is now a sizable park featuring campers, a beach, and trails.

The Jamestown colonists' original landing place is close to the Cape Henry Lighthouses, two recognizable lighthouses. For breathtaking views, climb the more recent lighthouse.

Military Aviation Museum: This museum is a sanctuary for aviation aficionados and is home to one of the biggest private collections of military aircraft from World Wars I and II.

The city's artistic energy is displayed in the ViBe Creative District with murals, galleries, and shops.

Every visit is distinctive since Norfolk and Virginia Beach each host a wide range of annual events, festivals, and concerts. These two cities guarantee enriching experiences for any visitor, whether they choose to immerse themselves in the history, appreciate the art, or simply enjoy the sun on the beautiful beaches.

Don't miss out!

Visit the website below and you can sign up to receive emails whenever Henry Church publishes a new book. There's no charge and no obligation.

https://books2read.com/r/B-A-GDIAB-NOXNC

BOOKS2READ

Connecting independent readers to independent writers.

Also by Henry Church

American Cities History Guidebook Series
Charlottesville, Virginia: Historical Guide for Travelers
Williamsburg, Virginia: Historical Guide for Travelers
Richmond, Virginia: Historical Guide for Travelers
Norfolk & Virginia Beach: Historical Guide for Travelers
Winchester, Virginia: Historical Guide for Travelers
Baltimore, Maryland: Historical Guide for Travelers
Dover, Delaware: Historical Guide for Travelers
Arlington, Virginia: Historical Guide for Travelers

About the Publisher

Fiel LLC is dedicated to providing high-quality content at affordable prices, utilizing state-of-the-art processes and advanced content generation systems to ensure a superior reading experience. All books published by Fiel LLC are for entertainment purposes only. Fiel LLC authors use pen names and are not experts in any field, so no content should be taken as financial, medical, legal, or professional advice. All information provided is subject to change, and readers are encouraged to verify the latest details through their own research.